To Ana,

THINK
Yourself™
SUCCESSFUL

by
Nathalie Plamondon-Thomas
Maureen Hagan
Tasha Hughes

You are
Awesome!

Nathalie

Disclaimer: The information in this book is for entertainment purposes only and does not constitute health advice in any way. Readers should consult with their own medical professionals before embarking on any health or mindset training.

Published by Prominence Publishing. www.prominencepublishing.com

The co-authors of this book can be reached as follows:

Nathalie Plamondon-Thomas: www.dnalifecoaching.com
Maureen Hagan: www.mohagan.com
Tasha Hughes: www.tashahughes.com

ISBN: 978-1-988925-01-1

First Edition: July 2017

PREFACE

A BOOK BY WOMEN, FOR WOMEN

This is a book written for women, by women. Even a quick perusal of the bookstore shelves or a Google search will largely produce literature about success (written by men). A book for men, who are neurologically hard-wired differently than we are, will focus on different issues. We can absolutely gain from the wisdom of our male counterparts, but a woman's process is different.

Writing for women has allowed us to address the emotional/mental content of the problems women face in their business, with the freedom to write authentically for our own gender. Our 'process' is about helping women to land in and live in their "sweet spot" mindset, and LAYER success on top of that.

TABLE OF CONTENTS

PART 1:
THE
INTRODUCTION

FOCUS &

WHAT'S IN IT FOR YOU?

GRANTING YOURSELF PERMISSION

THINK Yourself™ DNA System

save-on-foods #969
Ironwood
B.C. OWNED AND OPERATED
Visit www.saveonfoods.com
G.S.T #R846980878

Refund

$10

BALANCE DUE $10.75

$0.02

$11.00

CHANGE $0.25

****
As befits a More Rewards Cardholder
****
How was your visit today?
Tell us at www.saveonfoods.com/survey
and enter to win a $1000
Save On Foods gift card

OUR MONEY BACK GUARANTEE
return within 14 days of
purchase with original receipt
some restrictions apply

CASHIER Pharmacy 45
14:05:14   06Mar2018
0969   R045

CHAPTER 1

WHAT'S IN IT FOR YOU?

"Strength doesn't come from what you can do. It comes from overcoming the things you once thought you couldn't." —*Ashley Greene*

CAN YOU REALLY THINK YOURSELF SUCCESSFUL?

Can your brain really have anything to do with how you succeed? You may feel that success is only for others. Maybe you have an unconscious belief that, no matter how motivated you might be, you are just not able to engage people to buy your services, or have a company appoint you as their new CEO. This book is about to teach you how to change these limiting beliefs, to teach you about success itself, and how to program your brain to reach the heights to which you have always aspired.

It is no secret that the mind and the body are connected. The brain, being one of the most complex structures in the universe, has been the subject of studies and research for years.

THIS BOOK IS FOR YOU IF:

You feel that you are unsuccessful.

You feel deflated, and sometimes lose your motivation and confidence.

You have a hard time getting everything done. You think your busy schedule has control over you and you lack the discipline that would lead to sustainable actions.

You have a hard time staying accountable for the things you want to accomplish.

You sometimes feel like an imposter or a fraud, you feel ashamed, frustrated and wonder what's wrong with you.

You don't know where to start and feel like a beginner, you are lost and paralyzed, you have heard yourself say: "I don't know what I am doing.".

You hate selling or marketing yourself, you believe approaching a group is hard, and you think: "Why would they want to work with me anyway?".

You don't know where to start, who to call, what problem to solve first.

You can't seem to fit personal time into your schedule and when you do, you feel guilty.

You self-sabotage and find yourself not doing the things you are supposed to be doing, feeling that you are getting in the way of your own success.

You point the finger at yourself when facing challenges, letting your inside voice say, " I must suck then, it must be my fault", and you don't know how to stop the negative self-talk that is telling you to give up.

You keep your dreams on the back burner, you procrastinate and push off what's important to you to make room for what's important for others.

You have been successful but you have lost your mojo, you wonder how to get it back, along with your self-confidence, your hopes and beliefs.

Most of us see our lives going by without noticing. When we wake up one day and 10 years are gone, we say: "I wish I had done this, or that.", What is on the back burner? What are the dreams and hopes you put aside?

What do you want? What is your answer to the million-dollar question: "If you could do anything and be anything you want, what would it be? Our mind is very complex, but yet, quite simple. Whatever we dream, we can achieve. No mind will plant a seed unless it is able to grow the end result. So whatever your dream is, it is possible. Otherwise your mind would not let you even dream it.

In this book, you will learn about the D.N.A. System that Nathalie uses with her clients, combined with the experience and know-how of two successful women and co-authors Maureen Hagan, Global Fitness and Health Ambassador and Tasha Hughes, founder of Diva Defence and The Neuroscience of Thriving. Nathalie has combined her experiences as Business Owner, Sales Manager, Fitness Professional, Speaker, Nutrition Specialist, Life Coach and Master in Neuro Linguistic Programming, into a system that will show you how to reprogram your brain to succeed – and how to stay on the right track for good.

Collectively, we will share many examples with you about how our clients are being, and have been successful in changing their life from the inside out. It is a book about 'working in' vs. 'working out'.

In this book, we will review the components of success and help you define exactly what it means for you, in a way that will help you see the concepts differently, in a more mindful way. You will discover why your previous attempts to succeed may not have been as successful as you would have liked. In your DNA are the fundamental and distinctive characteristics that qualify who you are. Our most profound belief is that everybody has everything they need inside themselves. It is in your DNA. Somewhere inside, you know exactly what to do in order to be your best. We believe everybody is extraordinary and unique. Everyone can achieve the life that they desire. The know-how is all within you, waiting to be discovered.

The book is divided into seven major sections. The introduction, definitions of success, the factors causing us to fail, the foundation of the system as a general overview and one section for each step of the D.N.A. System to go deeper in details.

> *"You can't install new cupboards on top of existing cupboards. In order to get your brand new kitchen, you need to gut out the old stuff."*
> — *Nathalie Plamondon-Thomas*

This system is a key element of the THINK Yourself ™ Series. The structure of the system is quite simple. Pretend that you feel you need some changes in your home. You are not quite happy with some of the rooms in your house. You have some company coming in a few months and you would like to do a few upgrades.

The first thing to do is to assess what you want to spend your budget on first. What room will make the most impact and give you the most satisfaction? That's the DESIRE part of the D.N.A. System: finding out what you want to work on and what is your vision of the new room.

Now let's say you have decided to make changes to your kitchen. Before installing the new cupboards, you need to get rid of the existing ones. There is a demolition or a cleaning task to be done before putting the new cupboards in place. That is the NEW YOU part of the D.N.A. System. We clean up and get rid of old, unwanted emotions, behaviours and beliefs and make room for what you want to implement in your life.

Once clear and empty, all you need is to fill your kitchen with brand new cupboards and furniture, new paint, new floors, and whatever you have decided in your plan. The imprint and implementation of the desires into your new you is the ACTUALIZE part of the D.N.A. System.

The first step is to learn how the brain works and discover what you want, then you need to do some clean up, and finally you can install the new desires. You will discover the complexity and power of the brain and how to elicit what you want (desire). You will learn how to make room for what you want and some techniques to clear any negative impact from your past (new you). And finally, you will learn how to program your brain with what you want (actualize).

The D.N.A. System stands for: DESIRE - NEW YOU - ACTUALIZE.

We are addressing the internal journey of "Defining - Undefining - Redefining. We want to offer you a solution, an ability to 'change your state', a shift to 'BEING' Successful VS 'DOING' successful.

You will get a chance to practice the concepts right away in the book. We have included some brain exercises and techniques to start reprogramming your brain immediately. Nathalie has adapted some techniques that she has employed successfully with her clients into simple processes you will be able to use on your own. The exercises are there to help you start "THINKING Yourself™ SUCCESSFUL" right away.

You'll be amazed by your results as you apply what you discover in this book. Take the time to complete the exercises and with care and thought. After all, we suspect that this may not be the first book or tool you've purchased to boost your success. By making a commitment to embracing these exercises and this new way of thinking, this book will be the pivotal one in your life!

If you prefer to write your answers separately, you can download our free *THINK Yourself™ SUCCESSFUL* workbook at www.thinkyourselfseries. com.

You will notice lots of examples and sometimes repetition with the exercises. Change doesn't happen at a conscious level. Your logical mind (which we will explain further later on) is quite limited. Most of the processes you used before were based on your logical mind. However, change occurs at an unconscious level. You will discover how to get in touch with the most powerful portion of your brain: your unconscious mind. You know that we only barely touch the surface of the capabilities and potential of our brain. There is so much more we can tap into. Your unconscious mind will understand what we are talking about in the next chapters and will embrace these concepts. It loves repetition, just like a child who wants to watch the same movie over and over. Your logical mind might think, "... Really? That same question again? I answered that already. It is kind of the same question. Wasn't this concept covered already?" Well, while your logical mind is busy trying to think that way, your unconscious mind is saying: "Yay! I love this stuff, can I hear it again one more time, please?"

There are different reasons why people want to be successful. And there are many areas of success. In reading this book, keep in mind you can apply our system to any type of success, whatever success means to you. People associate success to different priorities. Nathalie coached a businessman who wanted to advance his career. As it turned out, he realized that spending time with his family was more important to him than the promotion for which he had been applying.

Most of the time people know the answers to their problems; they are inside their brains but are not revealing the solution. In the normal course of things, something happens and we respond. A problem is something that would not be a problem if we knew how to respond to it. We have to dig into our unconscious in order to find the solution. If we knew the solution right away, it would not be a problem.

Some people are just tired of feeling that they are not doing their best, some have decisions to make and are torn between two choices, some want to make changes in their lives, some sometimes wish they were different but they don't know what to change. The good news is they can be whatever they want to be.

Tasha believes success is an inside job. What we believe to be true about ourselves is projected onto the world around us, and then reflected back to us. This inner work is VITAL to our outer experience. We do not have to give our power away to outside influences. We can grab hold of the reins and design a life that is uniquely ours to design. Life will provide challenges and sorrows, but we can learn the skills to transform those challenges into gifts and compassion. We can train ourselves to stop, pause and reset, pick up the pieces, and move forward. Often times, our greatest obstacles are our best teachers, as we come to learn just how resourceful we can be, just how much grit we possess, just how brilliant we can be once we get out of our own way. Tasha's Motto: "I win or I learn."

KEY CONCEPTS:

This book is for you if you are interested in success

D.N.A. SYSTEM
Desire. New You. Actualize.
Decide what you want. Make some room. Program the desires.
Define. Un-define. Re-Define

DISCIPLINE
Take time to fully understand and perform the exercises that will be presented to you.

CHAPTER 2

GRANTING YOURSELF PERMISSION

"The best gift you are ever going to give someone is the permission to feel safe in their own skin. To feel worthy. To feel like they are enough."
— *Hannah Breacher*

It is so foundational to our successes in every area of life to grant ourselves permission. Permission, first and foremost, to just be who we are, no apologies required. We are all a "work in progress", ever-evolving and growing. The expectations we place on ourselves to be perfect are counterproductive to the success we seek.

We also need to give ourselves permission to acknowledge where we have treated ourselves unkindly or critically, or allowed ourselves to be treated as 'less than'. It is important to do an inventory and a house cleaning of the situations and relationships, which do or do not support us as individuals, and our larger vision of our success.

Allowing ourselves to honestly SEE ourselves as we are is crucial to our growth and progress. We can be extremely good at seeing the negative and accepting other people's voices in our heads that show us where we are lacking, how we are not good enough or never will BE enough. Granting ourselves permission to even look at these situations takes vulnerability and courage.

It also takes courage to see our own beauty, our strengths and all of the things we do right. A strong Sense of Self and a positive Self-Identity will support and fuel our present and future success in all areas of our lives. By the end of this book, if you give yourself permission to commit to this process fully, you will see positive change, you will experience a greater sense of freedom and more power over your choices. You will have a stronger and clearer vision of the New You, and you will have the tools to take you there!

If you prefer to write your answers separately, you can download our free *Think Yourself Successful* workbook at www.thinkyourselfseries.com.

Give yourself permission to Have Fun on this journey of self-discovery!

KEY CONCEPTS:

GRANTING YOURSELF PERMISSION

It takes courage to see yourself for who you are and trust that this journey of discovery will lead you to who you really want to be.

CHAPTER 3

FOCUS & BALANCE

"Success demands a singleness of purpose." — *Vince Lombardi*

Dedicate your focus. This book will take you on a journey to success, inviting you to reflect on yourself in a deep way, offering you processes, activities, tips and tools to use as you climb. As you are starting to read the book now, start with identifying one part of your life that you will focus on when you do the processes and activities suggested in this book. This chapter will allow you to split your life into eight segments. You will then choose a segment and keep it for the remaining of the book. For example, when answering questions throughout the chapters in the book and when completing the Style-LIST Personality Profile, ask yourself in what context you want to answer these questions and stick with this concept for the whole book. You can re-do all the exercises again, once you have completed and are successful at that one thing. Choose another context and then repeat so that you can become successful at this other area of your life. One thing at a time.

Imagine a professional tennis game where you could change a few variables: first, the number of balls used in the game and secondly, the number of opponents one should face at the same time. Pretend for a second that you are watching this tennis game where one of the each firing 2 or 3 balls at him. Can you see the chaos?

If people have too many balls in the air at once, they drop them. People who want to make changes in their lives start off highly motivated, and often have too many goals at once— change career, start a business, lose weight, get divorced, quit smoking, etc. If you try to address everything at once, it doesn't work. You get overwhelmed, which leads to depression and feeling badly. Your brain reminds you of the negative feelings when it hears the words success or career.

> *"Multi-tasking is great in the kitchen when you are trying to time the chicken to be ready at the same time as the potatoes. But do not assume it is a great way to manage a workday."*   — Joanne Tombrakos

The following exercise will help you with dedicating your energy to one goal. By doing one thing at a time, you will have a much greater chance of getting positive results than if you try to change everything at once.

If you prefer to write your answers separately, remember that you can download our free THINK Yourself™ SUCCESSFUL workbook at www.thinkyourselfseries.com

DIVIDE

You are now invited to divide your life into eight segments. While you may think that your life is separated into two—work and family—there are many other areas that influence your life. There seems to be a misconception of the word BALANCE. Since most people think that there are two components, family and job, isn't it uncanny that everybody talks about finding balance between these two things?

Think of your life as a pie chart with many slices such as career, love life, family, health, etc. It might be that one area of your life (one slice) doesn't make you happy and this will interfere with your success plan. Rate each area of your life from 1 to 10, reflecting how happy or not you feel in those sectors. If you see an area that's only 3 or 4 out of 10, you might chose to fix this area before you start your success plan. Work on one area at a time. If a wheel isn't balanced, the ride will be bumpy. Remember to write the numbers that you feel best represent your current state. Avoid thinking about what others would think of what your number should be.

For instance, a woman who does not have a significant other gave herself a 10 for *Love and Romance*. She was absolutely fine being by herself. That is what was okay for her, in her representational system, at that time of her life. If we had asked her mother, the mother would have probably given her a 1 out of 10 for *Love and romance*. It is not about how other people feel about each segment. It is about you. Same idea with a client who was making $25,000 per year who gave herself 8 out of 10 for *Money*. That was all she needed in her own model of reality.

Feel free to rename the segments if the label doesn't fit in your life and you would rather see something else there. The top part of the wheel, including Fun & Recreation, Love & Romance, Personal Growth, Health & Fitness,

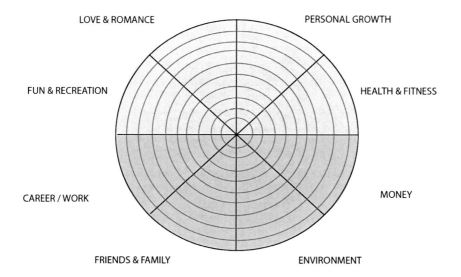

are connected to the primary needs of a human being. While the bottom part represents other areas of human life, these are important but not as vital.

Addressing the top part of the wheel is often a priority when working with this tool. Usually, when we fix our primary needs, the other areas of life can be met naturally as a by-product. For example, if you try to work on your environment or your career (which are two segments from the bottom part of the wheel), it may be difficult to focus on these if you are violently ill (Health and Fitness) or married to an idiot (Love and Romance)! LOL! Working on Love and Romance, Health and Fitness, Personal Growth, and Fun and Recreation will very often result, as a by-product, in embellishing the rest of the wheel. All the money in the world with the nicest house and the best career in the world will not make you happy if your primary needs are not met.

> *"Things which matter most must never be at the mercy of things which matter least."*   — *Goethe*

Once you have given a number to each segment, make a line representing the number, and colour the area from the centre of the wheel up to the line. That will look like this:

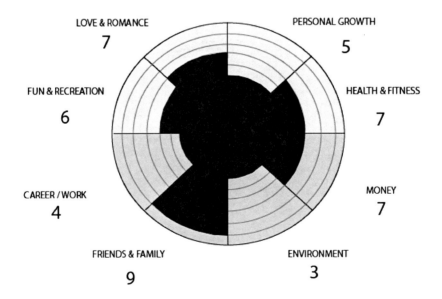

Pretend that you are a truck and that you roll on these wheels. Do you think that the road might be a little bumpy? The bumps in our journey are caused by imbalances in the different areas of our lives. It is because of these differences that deceptions and dissatisfaction are troubling us.

Nathalie once had a client who filled out the wheel and gave herself a three in all the segments, but one where she had a seven. This was a recent seven. A few months back, she would have given herself a three in all segments. She told Nathalie that she had been in a rut for years. Her ride was smooth. She had a constant three.

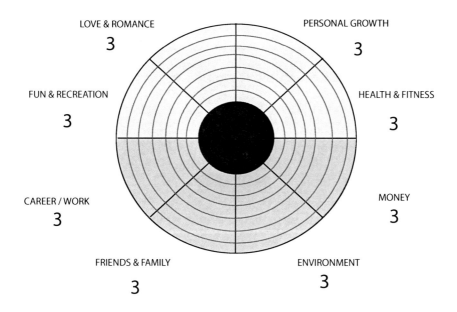

That made the wheel quite small and she was not going very fast, but she was not even noticing that all the areas of her life were not satisfying because there was no bump in the road to make her realize the differences. When she suddenly improved one part of her life that received a seven, she realized she had been missing out on everything else and it gave her the trigger she needed, and that is when she found Nathalie's website. We worked on each segment one at a time and after addressing only three segments, somehow, all the segments had improved. They are all interconnected.

Now think about your results and have a closer look at each segment. Try to identify the connections between each and every one of them. Because this book is about success, let's focus on the career segment of the wheel. What other segment is connected to it? Let's say that if you work on your personal growth, you'll acquire the skills you need to achieve your career goals, and then your money segment will also be affected. Or if you get out of an abusive relationship, you might find the self-confidence you need to make better choices. Or if you take more time for friends or health and fitness, you will reduce stress. You may have a much more pressing matter to address before being able to focus on your success.

Some areas influence others. Which area(s) of your wheel influence(s) your success?

_____

Which one do you want to address first?

_____

Now that you have identified which area of the balance wheel you want to work on, you are now ready to determine what you want and what is your desired outcome regarding this area of your life.

Once you go through the D.N.A. System with that area of your life, you can start over and choose another area. You can also elect to redefine and create a more focused wheel that addresses all areas of that segment.

For example, for a personal growth wheel, you can have the following segments: Time for myself, sleep, learning, meditation & spirituality, access to a mentor, do something unfamiliar, bravery and courage, negative emotions.

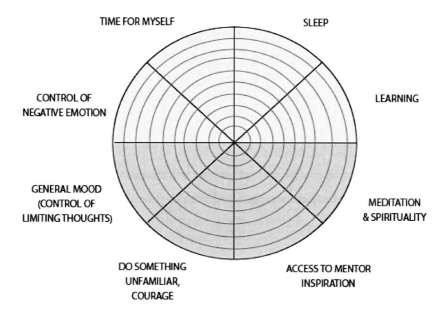

For a love and romance wheel, you can have the following segments: Time together, time apart, complicity, attraction, sex, day-to-day common life, collaboration, communication.

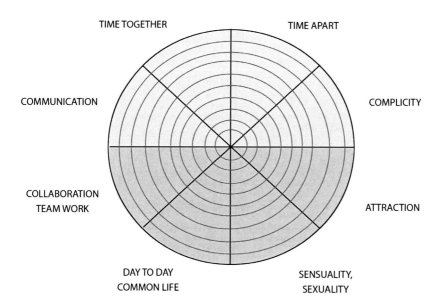

For a career wheel, you could have the following segments and work on one of them at a time: Use of my Skills, Co-workers, Clients, Achievement, Salary, Day-to-day Tasks, Number of Hours at work, Diversity, etc.

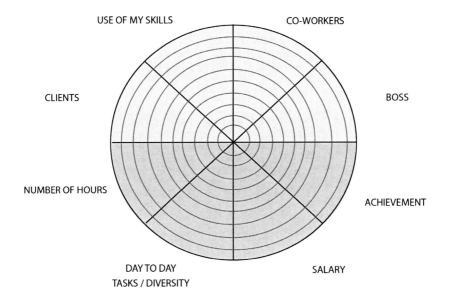

You can go on our website www.thinkyourselfbooks.com to download our free assessment wheels.

Now that you have identified what segment of your life you want to be successful in, let's look at success itself. What is it?

KEY CONCEPTS:

DEDICATE

Focus on one thing at a time. Address the main area of your life first, choosing the one that will have the most impact on the other segments. When answering the questions and doing the activities presented in this book, remember to stick to that one area of your life. Once completed, you can then address something else and re-do the exercises, answering other areas of your life.

PART 2:
SUCCESS

CHAPTER 4

WHAT IS SUCCESS?

"Success is not to be pursued, it is to be attracted by the person you become." — *Jim Rohn*

Success ultimately is how we feel about ourselves. How do we measure up to our own standards and our own definition of success? Certainly, there are those for whom nothing will ever be enough, and the quest for success will always be an evasive experience because no amount of money or status or material "stuff" will feed the underlying fear that "I am not worthy. I am not good enough."

That is why we consider success to be an inside job. Success is not something we reach or something we have, own or collect. Success is a feeling. We hope in these pages to help you on your journey of self-discovery, to align with your own truest definition of success, not someone else's. Success is less about what you do and more about how you do it and how you feel while doing it.

If the tasks you undertake and your negotiations and relationships with others demonstrate your character, integrity and caring, you are already successful, despite outward definitions. People will trust you, and therefore any undertaking with which you associate yourself (business, co-partnerships, new avenues). If you wish to layer on more, such as MASSIVELY ABUNDANT, SUCCESSFUL AND HAPPY, the only thing stopping you is sitting in your chair!

There is only one YOU, and your path or paths to success will be as unique as you are. No one else has your family and life experience, and therefore, your perspective. No one else has your exact career history and therefore your exact skillset. No one else has your brain and therefore your genius. As you delve further into the journey of your own success, ASSUME that you are a genius ... and then watch the magic unfold from there.

> *What is Success?*
> *To laugh often and much;*
> *To win the respect of intelligent people*
> *And the affection of children;*
> *To earn the appreciation of honest critics*
> *And endure the betrayal of false friends;*
> *To appreciate beauty;*
> *To find the best in others;*
> *To leave the world a bit better,*
> *Whether by a healthy child, a garden patch*
> *Or a redeemed social condition;*
> *To know even one has breathed*
> *Easier because you have lived;*
> *This, is to have succeeded."*
> *— Ralph Waldo Emerson*

Success is achieved when people are in touch with their deeper structure, when they control their emotions and find alignment within themselves.

Success is to align every layer of our own self, in order to find our life purpose.

The layers of a person's self represent the base of this book and the foundation of the DNA System.

Success is to live in an environment that serves us, with behaviours that use our skills or build them, as we follow our own beliefs and values to live our full identity and reach our life purpose.

We will explain each layer in detail, along with what happens in our brain at every level. We will get back to the pyramid throughout the book, working on each level, along with the D.N.A. System, which will lead us to reaching our life purpose and wisdom.

Success is to live a fulfilling life and to be our own personal best! You will learn a lot about yourself and mostly, you will learn that your personality is not set in stone and that you can become whatever you want to be.

Let's have a quick overview of specific characteristics that successful people have in common.

KEY CONCEPTS:

WHAT IS SUCCESS?

Ultimately, success is achieved when we align and integrate all layers of our own self in order to achieve our life purpose and gain wisdom.

The whole book is designed to take you on a journey through the neurological levels of your brain, embarking on the D.N.A. System that will carry you through each level and allow you to reach your full potential.

CHAPTER 5

COMMON SUCCESS TRAITS

"Never water yourself down because someone can't handle you at 100 Proof." — *Unknown*

As defined in the previous chapter, success is internal. Success is part of who we are. Let's have a look at characteristics that successful people seem to have in common.

Mo mentions how lucky she is to be surrounded by inspiring and motivational women who have helped her shape her career and the type of leader she has become. She says to all young graduates: "I've always lived by the mantra that the workplace is an equal playing field… but you've got to earn it. My advice to you is: hard work and dedication do pay off. If you work hard, you will be successful in which ever career path you choose."

The following are her personal experiences and tips that have helped her get to where she is today. We will teach you later how you can apply these, and become the powerhouse woman we know you can be!

NETWORK WITH OTHER THOUGHT LEADERS

If you want to be successful in your given field, get to know the people who are already successful. Surround yourself with like-minded people you look up to and soak in everything they say and do. Better yet, ask them to grab a coffee, pick their brain and learn from them. Building a relationship with a variety of people who inspire you is key to developing your own skills and approach. There is a reason you look up to these people but make sure you're not 'looking' from afar–use every

opportunity you can as a source of knowledge that can help guide you through your professional endeavours.

Mo's mentors are passionate and hardworking. They are women who have helped shape the fitness industry, and transformed it from the traditional 'old boys club' to what it's become present day—a gender-equal place of opportunity. Women who love what they do, have a combination of education and self-taught business knowledge and have reached impressive heights in their careers through hard work and dedication. These are the women we always feel inspired by.

> *"You can't put your hand in a bucket of glue without some of that glue sticking."* — Jack Canfield.

These are some of the fantastic women that Mo looks up to:

Deborah Sienna – Lynne Brick – Helen Vanderburg – Sara Kooperman – Lexie Williams – Jane Riddell – Barbara Klein – Tosca Reno –Silken Laumann – Petra Kolber –just to name a few.

TRAITS FOR SUCCESS

All different, but all well respected women in their own right, each mentors have enviable qualities that no doubt have helped them further their career. Here are some common traits found amongst the most successful women (and men too) that we know:

PASSION

Being in a field you are passionate about is one of the most important elements to success. Life is too short not to love the work you do. If you truly love your job, it will shine through.

> *"There is no passion to be found playing small - in settling for a life that is less than the one you are capable of living."*   — *Nelson Mandela*

CONFIDENCE

Attitude, attitude, attitude! Having confidence in yourself and the work you produce is important. If you know you can do the job and you know the work you produce is valuable, act like it. You have to believe in your skills, goals and ability to succeed. If you believe in yourself the success will come in due time.

> *"The most beautiful thing you can wear is confidence."*   — *Blake Lively*

RELATIONSHIPS

We already touched on getting to know your mentors. Networking as a whole goes hand in hand with workplace success. It's not all about who you know, but it certainly helps, especially when you have great people vouching for you.

> *"You can make more friends in two months by becoming interested in other people than you can in two years by trying to get other people interested in you."*   — *Dale Carnegie*

EMPATHY

As women many of us have a nurturing side. Empathy is having the ability to put yourself in someone else's shoes and understand their situation and feelings. Having empathy makes you a great leader, as you are able to see the whole situation, not just one point of view.

> *"When you start to develop your powers of empathy and imagination, the whole world opens up to you."*   — *Susan Sarandon*

DRIVE

Having the determination to work harder and get things done is probably the key ingredient for success. A great work ethic combined with that positive attitude I've been talking about goes a long way.

> *"I didn't get there by wishing for it or hoping for it, but by working for it."*   — *Estée Lauder*

TAKE RISKS

Don't be afraid to take risks, stand up for what you believe in and go after what you want.

> *"If you don't risk anything, you risk even more."*   — *Erica Jong*

These are common traits for success in any industry. Whether you see yourself becoming a writer, a doctor, an accountant or a fitness professional, these traits are universal and won't go unnoticed.

Now that we have an idea of what success is and common success traits are, let's look at the factors that contribute to create imbalances in our life.

KEY CONCEPTS:

COMMON SUCCESS TRAITS

Network with other tough leaders will teach you how they created their success.

Passion, confidence, relationships, empathy, drive and taking risks are common traits of successful women that inspired us.

Identify with others who inspire you to help you clarify your own success strengths.

PART 3: OBSTACLES TO YOUR SUCCESS

CHAPTER 6

WHAT CAUSES OUR PROBLEMS?
IS IT FEAR?

"Your Mission: Be so busy loving your life that you have no time for hate, regret or fear." — *Karen Salmansohn*

THE FEAR RESPONSE

Your body will alert you to possible danger, shooting you a burst of adrenaline so you can run away from predators, fires, floods and other life-threatening events. This response was useful thousands of years ago when man was at the mercy of wild animals.

Neuroscience sheds some insight as to how our brains are hard-wired to sometimes experience fear and interfere with our goal-seeking efforts, and why improved action can be so difficult to maintain.

The most ancient part of our brain is the centre of our survival area (the amygdala), also known as "fight or flight" response, more recently and accurately described as "fight, flight or freeze." Each individual will have a different response to a threat or a stressor, which falls into one of these three categories. The job of the amygdala is to guard our safety and self-preservation, but it also holds the key to understanding why we sometimes choose seemingly self-destructive patterns, when our desire is actually to move in a new direction.

As an example, a group of friends decide to partner up in January of the coming year to help each other lose weight and hold each other accountable. As will often be the case, one of the members of the group may have a faster and easier time attaining results than the others. These quick results may be met with both encouragement from members of the group, but possibly also negative feelings from others whose results are not so quick. The amygdala of the person who is having the better results will assert itself and say: "Danger, danger … you are separating from the group and threatening your sense of safety." Before you know it, this friend 'falls off the wagon" and has one too many wine-soaked nights, or indulges in snacking with the kids in the name of fun, all in order to maintain her sense of safety and belonging within the group.

After reading this book, you will recognize when the amygdala is in charge, and retrain your brain to reframe your circumstances. This will allow you to leap beyond your present limitations. This book will help you rethink your definition of your comfort zone, helping you and your brain move beyond fear into exhilaration!

> *"Everything you've ever wanted is on the other side of fear."*
> — *George Addair*

We were called to write this book because we are each very familiar with experiencing fear in our everyday lives. It would be a mistake to think that successful people are never afraid of anything. Fear is present for each of us. Nathalie did not always feel great about standing in front of an audience. Her first real appearance was in grade 7 performing an exposé in front of her class. She recalls: "As I stood in front of my classmates, I completely forgot my text. I had no idea what my subject even was and I ran out of the class in tears. I was so humiliated. Even after the teacher insisted I complete the assignment, giving me a day to rehearse, the same thing happened the next day (although at home I was totally nailing it!). I did not know how to deal with this fear. My parents signed me up for a personality contest, teaching me that everything can be learned and that we can overcome a fear of anything. I managed to face my fear of public speaking after hours of rehearsing and mastering techniques to gain my confidence. I now continue to practice and acquire techniques and skills that allow me to make a living of public speaking."

> *"We need to accept that we won't always make the right decisions, that we'll screw up royally sometimes—understanding that failure is not the opposite of success, it's part of success."* — *Arianna Huffington*

We will not teach you how to not be afraid. Instead we will help you see challenges as opportunities to grow and explain how to train your brain to exit the emotion instead of being stuck in it.

FEAR is an emotion. We experienced it for the first time between the age of zero and seven years old. When it happened, just like any other emotion, we entered an emotional loop which can last from thirty to sixty seconds. At the end of the loop, we unconsciously choose to stay and re-enter the loop or to exit it and move on to go back to a neutral state. When we experienced it for the first time, as a child, maybe because we heard a noise in the middle of the night, our unconscious mind came to the rescue and took the emotion away from us so that we could go back to sleep. It placed the emotion somewhere in our unconscious mind and created a thread on which a pearl would be added every time fear would appear in our life. With time, we accumulated a long pearl necklace of fear, which can contribute to feel like we are struggling with fear for no reason. With a long string of fear, we tend to stay in the negative emotion loop much longer than necessary. In order to decrease the length of our necklace along with our susceptibility to experience this negative emotion, we can look back at the specific times when fear appeared to be an issue in our life and make this pearl disappear by acknowledging what we have learned from this specific event.

Each challenging event in life presents itself in order to make us grow. It comes with a positive learning. Now just like the tasteful avocado flesh comes with a pit, the positive learning comes with a negative emotion. In order to get rid of the pit, we must go through the flesh. We need to acknowledge what we have learned in order to be able to let go of the negative emotion. As soon as we understand that we are on a journey of growth filled with learning opportunities, we can easily let go of fear or other negative emotions that we have accumulated in our past.

Once you work through the specific events that contributed to build your fear necklace and learn how to look for the positive learning behind the challenges you are facing, you can free yourself from these negative emotions.

We will learn more specifically in the NEW YOU section how to get rid of these negative emotions and create a habit so that in the future, when you face a challenge, you immediately enter the event and look for the positive learning which will help you discard the negative emotion right away. So it's not that you will never enter the loop again. You will just have the resources to exit it very quickly. You will have access to a different part of your brain, where you will create a shift and allow you to clear your mind and make an enlightened choice.

Today fear is more of a signal to stay alert and aware, but not to run away from it. Jack Canfield compares fear to a toddler who doesn't want to go grocery shopping with you. Would you let a toddler mentality run your life and keep you from going grocery shopping? You need to have food in the house, so you need to take the toddler along with you. Of course your other option is to let your toddler stop you from going. Eventually you will go hungry. The ideal response to fear is acknowledging and experiencing it. As author Susan Jeffers suggests: "feel the fear and do it anyway."

In the theory above and in Nathalie's fear story, we have learned that fear can be faced with practice, repetition and the acknowledgement of positive learning. Tasha's fear story below will now shed light on how our true values can save us when fear strikes. Circumstances can change, but the values are always there; "When I knew my marriage was falling apart, I was full of fear; fear that I had failed, fear that we had failed the kids, fear of life not turning out according 'to plan', fear of what people would think, and fear about what the future would hold for all of us.

When I finally accepted that there was no turning back, I realized that what I feared the most was not only the pain associated with all of the changes that it would mean for our family, but also the loss of love we would all experience as a result.

That realization caused me to really reflect on what I believed to be true about love. I truly believed that love remains, even when circumstances change; that love is a powerful force larger than man-made circumstances. That thought made me feel stronger. Bit by bit, I replaced fearing the loss of love, with love itself. That is when the healing began, and I found the courage to walk a new path. Life continues to ebb and flow, but that powerful memory always helps to bring me back to centre."

Fear is also present when we compare ourselves to others and put unnecessary pressure on ourselves. When Mo was invited to New Zealand to present in a video for an international fitness program, she said "YES" before fear set in. Here is her fear story: "I created pressure on myself to perform at my best. Even though I had been presenting at fitness conferences around the globe for decades and was confident about my presenting abilities, I allowed fear to interfere with my self-confidence. So much so, that I was not able to articulate and coach the basic choreography within days of filming. It was like I had never taught before. I was paralyzed. I even called my husband one night and said that I should just come home and quit teaching. I was reminded by the program coach that there were many reasons why I was selected to be there. That reminded me that I was there to share my unique style of teaching with the world, invited to simply step into the experience and to stand in my own power—not try to compare myself to others. I recognized how I was creating my own fear by fantasizing negative outcomes, and needed to flip the outcome to the positive."

Mo fondly recalls this experience and believes that she had that to lean into fear, in order to move towards success. She has learned that success comes from experiencing the fear but not allowing it to keep her from doing anything she wants or has to do.

> *"It's not the absence of fear, it's overcoming it. Sometimes you've got to blast through and have faith."*   — *Emma Watson*

Although there are lots of different causes, in more cases than others, fear is triggered by the unknown. When we are unfamiliar with something, we gravitate towards fear. In the next chapter, we will discover how the different stages of learning can help with our fear. By knowing where we stand, we can manage our fear, and be conscious of the fact that our "unknown" is about to become a "known."

KEY CONCEPTS:

THE FEAR RESPONSE

FEAR is our body's way of keeping us safe. However, most of us, at least anyone reading this book, is not under a daily threat of lions, tigers and bears.

Often, fear stands in our way. Fear keeps us in our comfort zone and aligned with the familiar. When we want to pursue success, fear can inhibit our best efforts.

CHAPTER 7

THE FOUR STAGES OF LEARNING

"Success is no accident. It is hard work, perseverance, learning, study-ing, sacrifice and most of all, love of what you are doing or learning to do." — *Pele*

Now that we have identified that we fear what we don't know, we can teach you how the four stages of learning, and identifying at which stage you are presently, will contribute to reducing your fear.

All behavioural changes and lessons learned are unconscious. Unconsciously, we go through four phases. Early in the process we experience fear. That's when we need to channel our energy and be brave and/or persistent.

UNCONSCIOUS INCOMPETENCE

At first, we don't know what we don't know. We think being successful must be hard. This is the stage of *unconscious incompetence*. We have great news for you. As you are reading this book, you have already stepped over that stage. This is the first day of the rest of your life. You can never go back to not knowing what you are about to find out. Your life will be changed forever! You will never be able to not know this anymore. You may have to work at applying all the techniques that we will show you, but you are not unconsciously incompetent anymore because you have been made conscious that these techniques exist.

CONSCIOUS INCOMPETENCE

By being introduced to the idea that making money can be easy, we now know that it is possible. We are not skilled yet, but we know it can be done. This is the stage of *conscious incompetence*. We start practicing and learning.

> *"Not knowing you can't do something is sometimes all it takes to do it."*   — *Ally Carter*

CONSCIOUS COMPETENCE

Then it is *conscious competence*. Now we are good at it. We know what we are doing and our skills become habitual and consistent. We still have to consciously think about how to phrase our thoughts and how to apply the techniques that we have learned but they become very easy.

UNCONSCIOUS COMPETENCE

The last stage is reached when the skills become automatic. This is the ultimate goal. Once we are able to make choices without even noticing or thinking about it, we have reached the level of *unconscious competence*.

Have you ever been at the wheel of your car and arrived at your destination, and thought to yourself: "Am I already here? How did I even get here? I was not even paying attention." You don't have to think anymore about what to do when you see a red light or a green light, you just drive and know the route and everything is automatic.

> *"Every artist was first an amateur."*   —*Ralph Waldo Emerson*

The unconscious is where we can begin problem solving. Once we have done something for a while, we become unconsciously competent and collect unconscious skills. The problem is that we can develop bad habits that way, become discouraged or depressed, thinking that having success has to be hard, marketing yourself is tough, etc.

> *"One of the secrets to staying young is to always do things you don't know how to do, to keep learning."*   — *Ruth Reichl*

There are lots of things in our lives that we do automatically. We never have to pay attention while brushing our teeth in the morning. We just do it. In the same way, we are able to avoid doing lots of things because of the way our brain is programmed. For example, a person convinced they have a sweet tooth, will be able to avoid salty snacks very easily as they have programmed themselves to have a downfall for cake, and not for chips.

KEY CONCEPTS

THE FOUR STAGES OF LEARNING

When we know better, we can do better.

As we learn what we can do better, we have to pay attention in order to succeed at doing it, until we become unconsciously competent and we can succeed with our eyes closed, as a mechanical reflex, a habit.

CHAPTER 8

WHAT CAUSES OUR PROBLEMS?
IS IT STRESS?

"Every day we have plenty of opportunities to get angry, stressed or offended. But what you're doing when you indulge these negative emotions is giving something outside yourself power over your happiness. You can choose to not let little things upset you." — *Joel Osteen*

THE STRESS RESPONSE

Stress is both a biological and physiological response to a threat we have no resources or ability to master. The "stressor" or threat that causes stress, triggers the release of cortisol, a stress hormone designed to shut down non-essential functions and give us bursts of energy in the event of a lion, tiger or bear! Unfortunately, modern lives provide plenty of opportunities for increased stress and very little opportunity for relaxation and calm. Therefore, our stress responses are hyper-stimulated, with little or no reprieve. The body is under routine assault by metabolic processes intended to be life-saving, that ironically now contribute to the increase of disease and death in our culture.

If you are eating or digesting a meal and you receive a stressful phone call, the amount of cortisol released would be sufficient for you to run for your life. Immediately, digestion is halted and blood shunted away from the core to the brain and extremities to leave you free to respond. Consider how many meals in the course of a week, a month or a year are not digested properly due to stress. It is not a surprise to learn that our overall weight gain as a society, the increase in digestive issues, heart disease, and disease related to the processes of digestion and elimination is spiraling.

This is one of the reasons why relaxing times with family and friends, yoga classes, exercise and meditation are so crucial to overall health, as well as success. Creativity is also halted when the brain shifts into "fight or flight" mode. The antidote that will create balance, health, and ultimately success, is a conscious approach to mitigating the stress response and creating a supportive environment for ourselves.

If we look at it as a trigger for balance-seeking state, then we can use stress to our advantage and use it as an opportunity for growth. If we do not have what it takes to deal with the situation, we will build it, learn and grow.

PRESSURE VS. STRESS

What is the difference between pressure and stress?

Pressure is external. It is what happens to us in our lives. It surrounds us every day. It is our alarm clock not going off, it is traffic, it is running out of milk, our boss holding us accountable for extra work, our child not feeling well, an unexpected expense, one of our parents falling ill etc. So all that external pressure is presented to us every day and it is affecting us

This external pressure creates stress in our body. Stress is internal. A good way to get rid of stress is to take some time for ourselves and focus, meditate or have a good sweat! Any type of exercise will help us clear away the stress, momentarily. Yes, the external pressure will still be there, but it will not affect us for the time being. We will feel like a million dollars after we exercise and say to the external pressure: "Bring it on!!!." Later on, we will show you how to make this temporary stress-free state of mind last. You will learn how to let go of the built-up negative emotions that are really at the root of your response to external pressure.

Stress is related to success in the way that it impacts how we live our everyday life. It can be the element that keeps us from reaching our goals or not. As mentioned, stress is what we create and pollute our body with when we face external pressure.

TOO MUCH WORRYING

Stress is normally caused when we choose to worry.

Ninety-five percent of North Americans either go to bed or wake up worrying. As Isabelle Mercier says in #TEDxStanleypark: "Worrying is the #1 killer of creativity, performance and dreams." She feels we need to stop worrying because what we worry about is mostly nonsense or will likely never happen.

Forty percent of our worries will never happen. It's like putting a 40% down payment on a house you will never own…

Thirty percent has already happened, we just replay the movie in our heads.

Twelve percent are minor health annoyances such as light headaches.

Ten percent are miscellaneous, such as which shoes to wear.

Eight percent are legitimate problems.

So ninety-two percent of what we worry about is for nothing at all! We spend so much time dwelling on our problems that it becomes a habit to do so. We become good at having problems and if they go away, there is a sense of emptiness that we feel the need to fill with some other problems. Isn't that weird? Spend time focusing on what you want instead. The actual problem doesn't really matter. Make it disappear to direct y o u r energy into what you want. The actual problem doesn't matter. You have more likely made it up anyway. No need to dwell on it. Focus on the next step to get closer to what you want, instead of using your time worrying about what you don't want anymore.

If we can free up ninety-two percent of our "thinking-time", what should we do with our brain instead? How can we best put it to serve our quest to success? Let's have a closer look at the brain and how the different parts of our brains work for us or against us.

KEY CONCEPTS

STRESS RESPONSE

Stress is experienced when a "stressor" is applied to our lives and we feel we don't have the resources to respond. The key is to trust that everything that happens to us would not occur if we did not have the tools to deal with it. If not, that means the stressor (or external pressure) is happening in order for us to grow and build the tools we need.

PRESSURE vs. STRESS

Pressure represents the external reasons why we create stress inside our body.

We create our own stress when we choose to worry about the future, the past or about non-legitimate stuff.

TOO MUCH WORRYING

Ninety-two percent of what we worry about is non-sense.

CHAPTER 9

SUCCESS COMES FROM WITHIN

"Live Life as if everything is rigged in your favour." — *Rumi*

Your brain is the most complex structure of the Universe. Asleep or awake it controls every moment, every movement and every thought of your Life. Think about it: Do you have to tell yourself to breathe? To swallow? To blink? Your brain controls it all without you having to think about it.

THE LOGICAL MIND

We use our logical mind on the surface in our day-to-day. Your logical mind is the voice you hear in your head all the time. The one you use to make decisions. We actually give our logical mind lots of responsibilities and place lots of hope as to the extent of its power. The logical mind can process an average of between five and nine pieces of information at the same time. So while you are reading this book, you are more likely also able to notice an average of seven other things. For example, as you read, you can picture yourself understanding these concepts, you can see yourself in your suit on your way to sign an amazing contract, you can see what lays on your desk, hear if there is music playing in the background, notice that your pants feel uncomfortable, (and unfortunately depending on your actual programming and the way you think at this time), tell yourself that this book sounds too good to be true and that it will probably be another one of your unsuccessful multiple attempts to advance your career. You can do all of these things at the same time. Does it sound great? Your logical mind looks really powerful right? Just wait until you hear about the best part of your brain.

According to the research of Dr Raj Rahunathan Ph.D., we generate between 12,000 and 50,000 thoughts per day. Unfortunately, up to 70% of these thoughts are negative. We wonder what is wrong with us? Why is everybody else successful except us? We question why we haven't been chosen and tell ourselves we are probably not good enough. We think we would have time to focus on our own success if we didn't have to take care of everyone else. We think everyone is better and knows more than us. These negative thoughts, either looking for approval or control, or demonstrating feelings of inferiority, represent most our daily internal dialogue. Sadly.

When you start paying attention to everything you tell yourself, you realize why your efforts for success have been in vain.

> *"Would you want to be your friend if you talked to them the same way you talk to yourself?"*   — *Unknown*

Now, our logic might not be that great after all, right? And all these years, we solely relied on it for the most important decisions in our life.

Now the good news is that the voices inside your head have volume controls. You can make them louder, you can make them softer, you can make them say what you want to hear and in whatever tone of voice. We will learn all of this in the NEW YOU and ACTUALIZE sections of this book. For now, let's have a look at another part of your mind.

THE UNCONSCIOUS MIND

While the logical mind is busy talking down to you, the unconscious mind is busy working, understanding everything, down in the deep structure of our self. The unconscious mind can handle over two million pieces of information every second, (while our little logical mind was only able to hand seven, on average). Everything you have seen, done, thought, heard, felt is organized in your deeper structure waiting for your recall. Your unconscious mind sees everything. It reads all the signs and advertising while you drive to work. It hears every conversation around you, whether you are paying attention or not. It feels all the non-verbal signs that others are communicating to you without their own knowledge. It captures all the "behind-the-scenes" details that the logical misses. It takes all the info, it deletes, distorts and filters everything to create your own model of reality.

Your unconscious mind has so much information for you. It is dying to tell you. The problem is that people are not trained to think with their unconscious mind. Before today, you might even have thought that the unconscious mind was a one-way drawer. You may have thought that the logical mind is the one we use for thinking and that the unconscious mind is the one we use for storing.

Have you ever lost something that you had in your hand minutes before? You know you put it somewhere. You start thinking with your logical mind and wonder where you put it? Where can it be? You had it just now? Where did it go? The reason you can't seem to find it is because you are asking the wrong part of your brain. Your logical mind was probably busy with six other things and did not notice what you did with it. You want to ask your unconscious mind. It knows. Always. After all, it was you that put it somewhere. You are not asking your unconscious mind to read somebody else's mind. Just yours.

> *"Whatever we plant in our subconscious mind and nourish with repetition and emotion will one day become a reality."*   — *Earl Nightingale*

RELAX AND ASK YOUR UNCONSCIOUS MIND

We could spend pages and pages giving you stories of our life as we are constantly using our unconscious mind to find things.

Tasha's son rarely needed to go to the doctor. One day, shortly after his birthday, which was also the card renewal time, he did need medical attention: "I repeatedly went through my wallet looking for the NEW revised card. I panicked, wondering where I put it when the new card had arrived. All I could find was the old one. Knowing that I could usually count on myself to "put things in a safe place", especially if it involved my son. I relaxed, did 5 minutes of yoga which helped to shift me into a different neurological state, and then looked in my wallet again. As it turns out, the card I kept passing by as the old one actually WAS the new one. In my state of panic, my brain was not allowing me to 'see' the new expiry date as the correct one. I was right, I can trust myself to put things in a safe place, but the wrong part of my brain was in control during those moments.

> "We cannot solve our problems with the same thinking we used to create them."   — Albert Einstein

ANCHOR AND REINFORCE

Mo faced an unfortunate situation in Melbourne, Australia: "I lost my wallet, all my ID, airlines ticket information, money and a gorgeous black pearl ring. This memory has been haunting my unconscious mind ever since."

Now, even over 25 years after it happened, when she thinks she may have misplaced her wallet, her first physiological response is to relive the negative emotions that were created the first time she lost her wallet. But instead of staying in that state of mind, she has retrained herself to stop from going straight into panic mode: "Instead, I breathe, I retrace my steps and have trained my unconscious mind to always find my wallet. I give myself a pat on the back when I manage it well, give myself a pep talk when I haven't managed the situation so magnificently and thirdly, I practice gratitude by thanking my unconscious mind. I have now trained myself to always put my wallet back in the same place in my purse every time."

Training your unconscious mind to talk to your logical mind whenever you need it is a great use of this amazing portion of your brain. Anchoring great habits and creating alternate positive behaviours is a tool you will learn later on.

Using the D.N.A. System, you can make your logical mind and unconscious mind communicate together so that you have access to that deeper structure, where everything is clear and simple. The answers are all within you, waiting to be accessed. In Tasha's care card example, she could have let stress and panic get in the way. She surely did for a few seconds. It is not that she never goes there. She just doesn't stay there long. With practice, you get used to exploiting the power of your unconscious. When the layers and layers of negative emotions and negative thoughts have been removed, there is a clear path between your logical and unconscious mind. The NEW YOU part of this book, the N of the D.N.A. System, will allow you to remove all the junk from the drawer so that you can access the amazing you at the bottom of it. This communication with your deeper structure is one of the most powerful techniques you will learn.

Work on changing the attitude: "if it happens, it happens" into: "it will happen because I will make it happen." It is time. If you are tired of feeling that you are not in charge of your destiny and tired of watching your life happening to you, if you are tired of having tried lots of methods to reach your goals, only to get a temporary boost and then get back to the same old rut again, this books is for you.

We have a passion for people. The power hidden in the words we use everyday is underrated. We will see in this book how we can use the power of words to serve our goals in life. So what's in this book for you? Power to think for yourself. We are not going to give you advice and tell you what to do. We will show you how to generate the solution yourself. People need to make their own decisions in order to stick with the consequences. Their own brain needs to generate the idea. So we don't give advice. This book is not about us but about YOU. You will find your own answers. We will ask powerful questions and help your unconscious mind to deliver to you the answer that will serve you best.

Have you ever told something to someone so many times and then 4 months later they have the brilliant idea of doing what you had been suggesting? You want to shake them and say: "Well, that is what I have been telling you to do for months!!!" But they were not listening. They have to be the ones getting the idea themselves. When you told them, at the time, their brain was not ready to process that information. Unless they generate the idea themselves, you can tell them all you want, but it isn't going to work.

Clients and friends often ask us for advice, or they want our opinion on something. The on-going response is always: "It doesn't matter what we think. It doesn't matter what anybody thinks. We were not there. We don't know all the details about this. We don't have your background, your experiences or your values. Why don't you ask someone that was there all your life; who noticed everything; who heard every conversation and even picked up on all of the non-verbal information not picked up by anyone else? Ask your unconscious mind. It knows exactly what to do. The best moment to do so is at night before you go to sleep. When you get into bed tonight, intentionally ask your unconscious mind to recall every piece of information you have on the subject and to give you a clear vision the next morning. It is important to ask your unconscious mind to do this WHILE YOU ARE PROFOUNDLY ASLEEP. (Otherwise, it could keep you up all night). You must specify that while your logical mind is recharging and getting long hours of rejuvenating sleep, you want your unconscious mind to work in the background and give you answers in the morning.

Nathalie often uses that technique when she knows she has a deadline to write an article or a specific task: "I ask my unconscious mind to write it overnight so that when I wake up the morning after, the words come easily and effortlessly to me. I even use my unconscious mind to pack before a trip. It knows every single piece of clothing I own, it knows which ones I prefer, which ones are the most comfortable and appropriate for the trip that is ahead of me,". Some people say that it can even tell the future and that it knows if it is going to be sunny or cold. So let your unconscious mind even pack for you. "Usually, the morning after asking my unconscious to make the list for me, I only need 15 minutes and my suitcase is closed!"

Imagine how great your life will be when you can access all the knowledge and the experience that your unconscious mind has for you! People always have all the answers to their problems within themselves and you are about to learn how to access it.

PEOPLE HAVE ALL THE RESOURCES THEY NEED TO SUCCEED.

This opens up possibilities. By resources, we mean the internal responses and external behaviours needed to get a desired response. Often people have resources that they haven't considered or are available in other contexts. Maybe you know someone who shows good leadership skills at work but can't manage his or her children. A lot of people are wondering why they can be so polite with strangers and yet, be so abrupt when it comes to talking to their spouse or partner. Why is it that we can have a skill - patience in this example - and not use it? If you have the skill you have it. It is like being pregnant. You cannot be pregnant just sometimes on some occasion. You are or you aren't. When you have a skill, you have it. It is there in your belly. Period. So if you can be patient with strangers, you can be patient with your partner. It is just a matter of re-wiring your brain.

All the capability is within us and is waiting to be discovered. Let's stop limiting ourselves. We all have what we need. Everybody has the internal brainpower and the capability if they put their mind to it. You don't have to wait…. you don't have to say, "When I get this, then I will do that." You have all the tools in your brain right now. You can be whomever you chose to be today. You don't need to read another book on branding. No more searching for the magic seminar that will provide you with wealth beyond your dreams. You have everything you need right now, inside yourself. When you follow this principle, you will trust that your unconscious mind will guide you to find the tools and present to you everything you need.

Keep your eyes open and trust your unconscious mind to show you everything you know and trust that it will make sure that you get introduced to the right people, the right material, the right ideas. When you set your unconscious mind on a mission, it keeps working for you in the background as you continue to live your life. It makes sure that things happen well for you. We will see in the next chapter how you can use your unconscious mind like you would use a personal assistant.

KEY CONCEPTS

WE HAVE ALL WE NEED

People have all the resources they need to succeed. You can stop looking for external solutions to your problems. It is all there waiting for you inside.

The logical mind can only handle 5 to 9 things at a time while the unconscious mind can manage over 2 million pieces of information per second.

We tend to only ask input from our logical mind, which is negative 70% of the time.

People don't tend to implement other people's advice. They need to generate the solution themselves.

We should ask our unconscious mind for answers. They reside inside us in our deeper structure, which can be accessed once all the negative emotions have been cleared.

If you want advice, don't ask around. Ask yourself.

CHAPTER 10

YOUR PERSONAL ASSISTANT

"Between the stimulus and the response, there is a space. In that space lies our freedom and power to choose our response. In our response lies our growth and freedom." — *Viktor Frankl*

Your unconscious mind can be used as a personal assistant. The first step is to know that you can actually demand your brain to accomplish your wishes. Whatever you tell your brain, it will happen. If you tell yourself you're living paycheck to paycheck, your brain will do that. It's like you're writing a software for your brain. You can decide what you want to be written on the software. It is like re-inventing your own "you". What are you going to be?

PLACE YOUR ORDER

Your personal assistant inside your head takes notes and makes sure that everything that you say or think gets done. It's like having a waiter in your head, standing with a note pad and running to the kitchen to place your order. Whatever you think or say will get cooked by the chef and brought back to you exactly how you ordered it. So you really have to be careful when you think and when you talk. Your personal assistant is always listening. If you wake up in the morning and look at yourself in the mirror and say: "Oh my! I look horrible! I look tired!" then you continue with your day saying to yourself that you feel so stupid, or inadequate, or you don't want to be stressed and you hate rushing everywhere. You let the voice inside your head tell you that you are a failure and a fraud and you even tell yourself to not forget this (maybe a folder you are supposed to bring to the office). All your brain can hear is: Horrible, Tired, Stupid, Inadequate, Stress, Rush, Failure, Fraud, Forget the folder, etc.

If we ask you to close your eyes right now and to NOT visualize Mickey Mouse wearing a yellow tuxedo standing on top of an elephant, did you see him? Of course you did. Even if we said: "Do Not visualize Mickey Mouse...." Your brain doesn't process negation. So you have to be careful! People sit in Nathalie's office all the time telling her they don't want to be stressed anymore, they don't want to be fat, they don't want to be impatient with their kids and they don't want to be rushing all the time!

It is like they are telling their contractor that they want them to paint their kitchen *not* blue. So what do you want instead? Use your brain wisely, think and say what you want, not what you don't want!

We often hear people say, "I wish I liked recruiting clients." Who told you that you don't like that? You did!! You own your brain and you can write fresh software for your brain. Have you heard people say: "I am very bad with names. I wish I was good with names." The answer is always the same: Why aren't you? Who decided that you were bad with names? Who made the call?

Some people say: "I am a morning person" or "I am a night owl." They conditioned themselves to be that way and they believe it. Nathalie says on the subject: " If I need to stay up late, then I am an evening person and if I need to get up early, then I tell myself that I am a morning person. I can be both. Whatever is serving me." If a thought is not serving you, change it! Just start believing you are good at remembering names, trust me, there is so much room in your brain, you remember a lot of things that you don't need, so why wouldn't there be room for a few extra names in there?"

The brain is very powerful. If you think that you can, you can. We all grew up with different patterns and we've been told these patterns for 20, 40 years. The good news is that we can rewrite these patterns. If you tell your brain you are willing to learn how it feels to be successful, it will make you stop wasting time on non-important tasks. It will teach you how to master the skills you need to reach your goals. You have to be careful how you talk to your brain. All you have to do is to demand. Do so and you will receive.

THE CHEF KNOWS HOW TO COOK

Sometimes, we undervalue our worth. We feel that we have to restrain our demands to what we know. We don't allow ourselves to dream too high because we don't actually know exactly how to get there. Let's go back to the example of the waiter awaiting your order at the restaurant. When you order something to the waiter, you don't necessarily need to know how to cook the dish you have ordered. You just placed your order. It doesn't matter if you have a clue or not on how to make the dish you want. The chef put it on the menu so that means that the chef knows how to cook it. The chef is your unconscious mind. It knows exactly how to make it happen. If you were able to dream it, it means that your chef knows how to cook it. You would not have been able to dream it if you did not have what it takes to realize it. All you have to do is to place your order with the waiter. The waiter will run to the kitchen and bring back your meal. When you are clear with what you want and what you expect from your unconscious mind, it starts working for you in the back burner while you continue to live your life. It guides you into being at the right place at the right time. It whispers answers to your ears when you are about to learn something that will generate results towards your goal. Trust that you have everything you need inside. You got this. Just place your order!

Now that we know more about the brain, let's find out about the components of the brain responsible for our programming.

KEY CONCEPTS

YOUR PERSONAL ASSISTANT

Your brain executes whatever you input into your software. All you have to do is dream and place your order to your unconscious mind.

If you can dream of something, it means that your chef knows how to make it happen.

CHAPTER 11

NEURAL PATHWAYS

"As a single footstep will not make a path on the earth, so a single thought will not make a pathway in the mind. To make a deep physical path, we walk again and again. To make a deep mental path, we must think over and over the kind of thoughts we wish to dominate our lives."
— *Henry David Thoreau*

So far, we have learned that fear and stress are in part responsible for blocking our success. We have also found out about the astonishing power of our mind, which controls everything happening to us. We will now connect the brain and how we have unintentionally programmed ourselves to self-sabotage. It is empowering to know that we are responsible for whether or not we are happy with our life. The good news is that it is not our fault. We have unconsciously developed negative neural pathways in our brain and we reinforce them every time we try something that does not work. Then we blame ourselves and feel badly.

Our brain's neural pathways are responsible for our self-sabotage. Let's say you live in a house surrounded by a thick cornfield. When you leave your house, there is no other path to follow except walking on the corn. You start stepping on it, and as you walk through the field, the corn bounces back up behind you. The second time you step on the same path, the corn bounces back up but it breaks a little and doesn't come all the way up. The third time, the corn is weakened even more, and so on, until, one day, you have a perfectly flat path in front of your house that leads to your preferred destination.

For now, unfortunately, when thinking about success, the only path you know leads to self-doubt and fear. As you continue to use your linguistic skills to change your thoughts, you will create new neural pathways inside your brain. That is how habits are created and formed. You will begin stepping onto a new path. This may feel hard at the beginning, as you have to break the corn to create the path, but once it's created and you have been there several times, the path will be clear and wide. With time, the old path will grow new corn and will not exist as a path anymore, and you will soon forget about the old route.

The pathway's information travels along through the neurons (nerve cells) of the brain and affects our memories. The more we review them in our mind, good or bad, the more deeply they are etched in our neural pathways.

Here is a quick exercise to take a neural pathway through a different route from an old one you have built throughout the years. If you're right-handed, try to write your name with the left hand, and vice versa. We know how to write it, and yet we can't do it very well with our left hand... but we could if it were really necessary. Create a new neural pathway by writing it with your opposite hand. It's not easy, but you can do it!

Write your name with your left hand, or reverse if you are a left-handed person:

_____

How did it go? It's amazing how we can learn whatever we want. You can re-teach your brain to do things differently. Just practice. Repetition. Repetition. Repetition.

Do you remember when you switched to your mobile phone? You had to learn a whole new way of phoning, texting, emailing, posting on social media . . . How about switching from a keyboard to a touch screen? You got this, right? You have learned, and you are now able to easily use your phone. All while you were trying to make your new phone work for you, there was more likely never an intention of returning to the flip phone right? You knew you would be able to learn it.

Success starts by *expecting* that you will be successful. Your chances of success rely on what you expect to happen. Let us introduce you to the notion of the placebo effect.

There has been diverse research conducted in Finland, Texas and Canada on knee surgery.[1]

There were two groups of people who had knee problems. In the first group, they performed the actual surgery on the patient and fixed the knee. In the second group, they didn't perform the corrective surgery but the patient did receive a surgical scar. They did not tell the second

---

[1] http://articles.mercola.com/sites/articles/archive/2014/02/07/arthroscopic- knee-surgery.aspx

group of patients that they were not receiving surgery. They thought that they had been fixed. Both groups reported less pain and more mobility with their knee, regardless of whether or not they actually had the surgery.

This is a demonstration of the placebo effect. Medicine describes the placebo effect as "a favorable response to a medical intervention — a pill, a procedure, a counseling session, you name it — that doesn't have a direct physiological effect."[2]

That change can be from spontaneous improvement, misdiagnosis, classic conditioning or subject expectancy. The power of expectancy is a favourable response to a medical intervention that doesn't have a direct physiological effect (i.e. a pill, a procedure, a counselling session).[3]

It sounds very easy doesn't it? Well it *is* that simple! None of these patients had received extensive training in how to re-program their brains and how to create new neural pathways when it comes to pain. But they were told to expect a different sensation when faced with the movement that used to cause them pain.

The processes and activities coming up later in this book contribute to recreating healthy neural pathways. The best way to heal yourself, or, going back to the subject of this book, to succeed in your success efforts, is to *expect* that it will work. Use the placebo effect to your advantage and tell yourself that you will be successful. Whether you THINK it is doable or not… you are right either way.

We all create new neural pathways all the time (without knowing it). Every time we chose a new habit and stick to it for a while, a new neural pathway gets created. We will see how this works in a few chapters when we teach you how to move from conscious incompetence to unconscious competence.

---

[2] http://www.health.harvard.edu/mind-and-mood/putting-the-placebo-effect-to-work
[3] http://www.health.harvard.edu/mind-and-mood/putting-the-placebo-effect-to- work

Perhaps you have tried every workshop on the planet; you may have been successful for a while and then lost your way. Why? Because you THINK of success as something you will achieve at the end. You THINK that it is a destination. You THINK that what you have to do to succeed is TEMPORARY. You THINK that you can give a big push right now because it is only for a short period of time, because once you are successful, you won't need to work as hard, and these measures you are putting yourself under are not sustainable. You THINK success is impossible for you, and so, before you know it, you find yourself giving up and you're back to old poor habits, because they are familiar and comfortable.

None of your patterns happened overnight. If you take sugar in your coffee, leave it out for about two months and you'll create a new neural pathway and you'll be used to your coffee without sugar. Habit is the key word. We want our success to be a habit, an everyday thing, and not an extreme temporary measure. We see that the behaviours we need to succeed are temporary, and yet, if we want something that will last, that becomes a new behaviour without effort.

At first we have to pretend until it becomes a habit, which can happen in 66 days. Pretend that you want to be better at planning your day in advance. Tell yourself: "I am willing to learn how it feels and how it looks to be a great planner." Pretend that you are great at planning until you actually become great at it. In the Actualize section of the D.N.A. System, we will teach you many processes on how to "pretend" and re-program your brain. For now, just know that to pretend is the key, until the new neural pathways are created. You choose, you decide. Change the way you think about success. Change the way you think about sales. Change the way you think about marketing. Change the way you think about money.

Let's look a little closer at self-sabotage.

KEY CONCEPTS

NEURAL PATHWAYS

Our brain executes commands as it is told how to respond, and reproduces the same response over and over until it is being taught a new path.

Our life experiences create automatic responses in our head. These automatic responses become habits.

We get what we expect will happen.

CHAPTER 12

SELF-SABOTAGE

"This could be the day you stop doing that self-destructive thing you do."
— *Unknown*

Neural pathways are responsible for our self-sabotage. There are a few components of self-sabotage that we will cover in this chapter.

CORE VALUES & INTENTION BEHIND THE BEHAVIOUR

The first one is the intention behind the behaviour. We initially self-sabotage in order to keep us safe and in our comfort zone. Most behaviours start with good intentions. Even the teenager who takes up smoking to belong in the group, even criminals usually start out with good intentions, and then go downhill from there.

Finding the intention behind the behaviour becomes quite relevant when it comes to getting rid of a bad habit. One of Nathalie's coaching clients wanted to quit smoking. All on his own he decreased his habit to one cigarette per day, but was unable to completely quit. It turned out— after asking the right questions during coaching sessions—that he had not yet accepted the fact that his father had passed away. His father was a smoker, so the cigarette was connecting him with memories of his father. He did not want to let him go. Finding the intention behind the unwanted behaviour

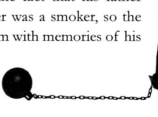

helps to find other ways to fulfill that positive intention. Now, instead of having his one cigarette at night (the unwanted behaviour), he takes out the photo album and looks at photos of his father so he can connect and honour his memory. He has been smoke-free for almost 8 years and is now running half-marathons.

Our cravings are often connected to deeper memories and triggered by our senses. We all know that certain smells remind us of certain things. Mom's cooking always made us feel good. Have you ever walked into a movie theatre or a bakery? You can smell the popcorn or the freshly baked goods, and immediately the cravings start. Find the reason behind the craving and then find a different way to fulfill that craving. If you miss your mom, call her or look at some pictures. You don't need to eat a whole chocolate cake because it makes you think about her. You can still think about her and love her without having to sabotage your health!

Here is another great example that shows how finding the intention behind the behaviour can help modify the behaviour. Nathalie had a client once who moved to a new city. All of a sudden she kept buying a certain type of chocolate bar and devouring it, and she couldn't understand why. Every day she needed that chocolate bar. She never used to like chocolate and it was never a problem before, even when she actually worked for the manufacturer of that particular chocolate bar. (which was quite ironic, a chocolate sales rep who doesn't like chocolate).

So why was she all of a sudden eating chocolate? What had changed? She called Nathalie and said: "Nathalie, you have to help me, I am eating chocolate every day and I am going out of my mind! I never used to like chocolate! What is going on?" After a few sessions, they realized she missed the life she had working for the chocolate company. She had moved and was now alone in a new city. Eating chocolate was her way of coping with feeling lonely and missing her friends. She didn't really want the chocolate bar; she wanted to be with her old friends. Now, instead of eating chocolate bars, she phones or connects with her friends on email or Facebook, which is a much healthier way to fulfill the intention behind her behaviour. She has gotten back to her healthy eating habits and is now in Australia, but she still keeps in touch with her friends on the web.

In order to discover the reason behind your negative behaviours, you want to ask yourself what it does for you. Here is an example of Nathalie working with a client:

> What does it do for you to procrastinate?
>
> *It allows me to do other stuff first and get rid of other pressing things in my schedule.*
>
> What does it do for you to get rid of other pressing things in your schedule?
>
> *It makes me feel like I accomplish stuff.*
>
> What does it do for you to feel like you accomplish stuff?
>
> *It makes me feel like I can do things, because usually when I procrastinate, it is for something that I am not really good at and it makes me feel inadequate.*
>
> So what do you want instead of feeling inadequate?
>
> *I want to feel successful.*
>
> And what does it do for you to feel successful?
>
> *It makes me feel like I am a great example for my kids.*
>
> And what does it do for you to be a great example to your kids?
>
> *It makes me feel like I am fulfilling what is important to me.*
>
> And what does it do for you to fulfill what is important to you?
>
> *It makes me feel complete and happy.*

So, in this example, the reason why this person would procrastinate is because she ultimately wanted to be happy and fulfill what she values most: family. So next time a task comes in and she feels like procrastinating, she will remember that at the end of the day, she wants to be happy and she is aiming to prioritize her family, which is what is important to her.

If it comes up in the process, it means it is really important to her . The thought of her family will give her the courage to embark on the task she was pushing aside.

We all have core values, which are the things most important to us. Often times, trying to align with the core values can be at the base of self-sabotage. When we are aware of it and can identify our core values, we can turn the situation around and make the core values the cure instead of the cause. Honesty, Family, Freedom, Respect, Certainty, Growth, etc. could be the values that take us out of self-sabotage.

Now it's your turn. Take a few moments to reflect on a bad habit that you would like to change.

"What does that do for you?" If your bad habit had a high intention for you, a high purpose, what would that be?

And then, use the answer to the question. What does that new answer do for you? What is its highest intention for you?

You can also use the following question if you go backward:

"What do you want instead?

Keep going with each answer until you find something that lights up in your head, until you tell yourself: " That's it!!! I get it!!!"

PAST EXPERIENCES CAUSING SELF-SABOTAGE

The second component of self-sabotage we will cover is how and why we continue to reinforce the behaviour.

"There is no failure, only feedback."   — *NLP Presupposition*

Every action we partake in generates a result. Whether it is a successful result or not, every attempt at success will generate a result. We hope it's a positive one but it may or may not work. Or it will work for a while and you may lose your ambition for a time. Your own past experience is there to teach you what did not work so that you can try something else. If nothing changes, then nothing changes. If you want to feel better and you need help getting motivated, this book is exactly what you have been waiting for.

If your previous attempts at success didn't work, then you need to receive feedback about why. Ask yourself what worked and what didn't work. Each action will give you a result. Success or not, whatever you do, you will obtain a result. Every action will give you information. This result will teach you a great deal about the action you performed. Was it successful? Did it work? Did it last? What can you do differently now to generate a different result?

Everything we do is only a trial. An experiment. We all have a certain percentage of success that follows us around. We all do things and we end up with a success rate of let's say 20%. That means that 1 action out of 5 generates a good reaction. The other 4 things are guiding us there. We are learning what doesn't work so that we can get to the magic 5th successful action. Every time we do something that doesn't work, that means that we get closer and closer to reaching the one that will work. Each move in our life is a stepping-stone towards something else.

Everybody we meet, every article or blog that we read, every action that we do, they are there temporarily to bring us to the next level. Living your life with this philosophy will help you respond better to what you viewed in the past as a failure. The next time something doesn't work out just say, "All right! That means that I'm now at three out of five and I have only two or more things to learn before I get it right!"

Repeat this: "I succeed at learning whatever I need to learn for my goal. I succeed at growing. I succeed at getting better and improving myself. Then I have another goal: To do it again and learn some more."

"Success does not consist in never making blunders, but in never making the same one a second time." — *Josh Billing*

It took Mo six months before she had the courage to send in her book outline to a publishing company: "Being a published author was one of my "big bucket" goals for 15 years. When a renowned publishing house approached me to write my book, you would assume I jumped at the opportunity. Well, I did initially, and within weeks I wrote the entire book outline, along with a number of chapters, but instead of sending it to the publisher for consideration, the manuscript sat on my desktop.

With each passing day I thought about my book, I became even more excited about it, then repeatedly talked myself out of sending it. Even I questioned what was holding me back, and with the help of my coach, I realized that it was my own negative self-belief and fear of rejection at play. I was recalling the past (as far back as high school), when I was criticized by my teachers for my writing and reading skills and cut from the team for lack of talent and ability. My coach helped me to see that by attaching a negative past experience (and perhaps an overprotective ego) to my intention, I was standing in the way of achieving my goal. Fear of criticism, fear of rejection by a top Canadian publishing house, and fear of failure were all at the top of my mind sabotaging my dream of becoming an author. With the help of my coach, I was able to refocus my thinking about the benefits associated with publishing a book, and to reflect on past experiences as lessons learned and opportunities gained."

One hour after she left her coach's office, Mo emailed her manuscript to the publisher. Within one week she received an invitation to meet with one of their editors. A few weeks later, Mo received a contract to write not one, but two fitness books.

Now when Mo is letting fear take over and self-sabotage set in, she is able to reflect and reframe her limiting beliefs. She will often think back to this experience when she is feeling unsure of herself. Mo still works with the same coach today.

LIMITING BELIEFS LEAD TO SELF-SABOTAGE

Have you ever felt like you dated the wrong guy? It's an experience most of us can relate to, and hopefully one we don't repeat often! Tasha had a client Sherie, who fell head over heels for the most amazing man. He was so perfect in every way. He always knew the right thing to say and the right thing to do. At first, he made her feel like a million dollars as he showered her with compliments, gifts and spontaneous romantic getaways. Sherie was an accomplished entrepreneur, confidently holding her own in her industry.

Over a period of time, Sherie changed from elated, strong and happy to more withdrawn, moody, and insecure. She began to defer to her boyfriend, valuing his opinion over hers. This started to impact Sherie's business. Her clients and employees had always known her to be self-assured and in charge, and they trusted her.

On some level, Sherie felt like a fraud. She had been told repeatedly as a child that her older brother was the smart one in the family. Her parents would ask why she couldn't be more like him. Why did she have to keep messing up in school and hanging out with the wrong kind of people? Sherie had these tapes running in her head; false ideas she believed to be true about herself. This is a perfect example of a few limiting beliefs that she cultivated all her life. They were installed by her parents at a very young age. Firstly, she believed that, in presence of men, she needed to give her power away. Secondly, she believed she would always meet the wrong people. She was programmed to not be strong with men and she was teaching them how to treat her. The limiting belief was unconsciously creating her self-sabotage.

When she wasn't in a relationship, she was "Strong and Confident Sherie," but with this man in her life, all of the old voices in her head started to play again. She found herself shrinking back in response to his success.

Sherie had given her power away. As a child she was conditioned to do so, and now she was repeating it with him. She didn't really feel worthy. She chose a man who actually fed off of her sense of unworthiness. Her choice of relationship was sabotaging her sense of self, and impacting the very thing that proved the voices in her head were wrong: Her business *and* her reputation as a strong leader.

The story has a happy ending. With strong support around her, she was able to see what she had done and why she hid in this relationship as a form of self-sabotage. Now she has rebuilt herself with the lessons learned, and is stronger and more compassionate than ever. She realized that changing her limiting belief was the key to stop her self-sabotage. She also chooses to believe now that she is attracting amazing people in her life.

OUR LANGUAGE LEADS TO SELF-SABOTAGE

Finally, let's talk about why we are giving in to self-sabotage. Why is it that, for some specific behaviours, like watching television or wasting precious time, we think that these behaviours are stronger than we are? We believe that social medias has power over us? It is just a question of programming. People keep programming themselves to be weak with some particular behaviours. They say: "Oh for me, selling is my downfall", or "Marketing is my downfall." So they are programming the brain that when they are selling or marketing, they will be weak and inadequate.

Doing tasks that bring us towards success should be exciting. It doesn't have to be boring either. There are some things you love doing. Things that you don't need any "willpower" to accomplish. You will learn to program your brain to start loving and being good at what serves your success.

When you waste time or self-sabotage your career, who gives the call? Who is asking you to do so? Your brain is. What if your brain were conditioned to be successful instead? Would it still give you the order to unleash these limiting behaviours? Why are you working against yourself?

You are self-sabotaging because you are focusing on the wrong thing: Not screwing up, not being stressed, not rushing all the time, not feeling inadequate, not feeling like a fraud. Your brain hears **stress, rush, inadequate** and **fraud**.

Clients sit in Nathalie's office constantly asking for the wrong thing. When she asks them how she can help them, their answer is usually focused on what they don't want. They say: "I don't want to be stressed anymore, I don't want to be rushing everywhere all the time, I don't want to be angry and impatient..." And the list goes on. It is like telling your general contractor that you want them to paint your kitchen NOT blue. So, the question is, what do you want instead?

You are starting to understand how this works, right?

You want to re-write your life. Create a new life, slowly, creating new healthy habits, rather than going on yet another "miracle project." How will you do it differently next time? You have been presented all the fundamental pieces you needed in order to understand the system we are about to introduce you. Turn the page and enter Nathalie's THINK Yourself™ D.N.A . System, fine tuned and improved with the precious collaboration of Tasha and Mo.

KEY CONCEPTS

Positive Core Values and Good Intentions can be at the root of self-sabotaging behaviour.

Identifying those values and intentions can help to turn the 'cause' into the 'cure'.

Past Experiences can cause self-sabotage. We can become conditioned through our life experiences to expect and accept that life will go a certain way and make our choices accordingly.

Our Limiting Beliefs can lead to self-sabotage. Our perception of ourselves and the world around us govern much of how we interact with people and situations.

Our language can lead to self-sabotage. We can become stuck in a bad feedback loop where habits and self-sabotage feed into each other. Creating healthier choices with our language can disrupt the feedback loop.

The way you think about success and your beliefs around your skills are causing you to self-sabotage your efforts to reach your career goals. YOU give the call.

PART 4:
THE FOUNDATIONAL LAYERS OF THE THINK YOURSELF™ D.N.A. SYSTEM

CHAPTER 13

THE NEUROLOGICAL LEVELS

"What lies behind you and what lies in front of you pales in comparison to what lies inside of you." — *Ralph Waldo Emerson*

After an overview of the common obstacles we face when aiming for success, and how our brain works, we are now ready to introduce you to the foundational pieces of our D.N.A. System.

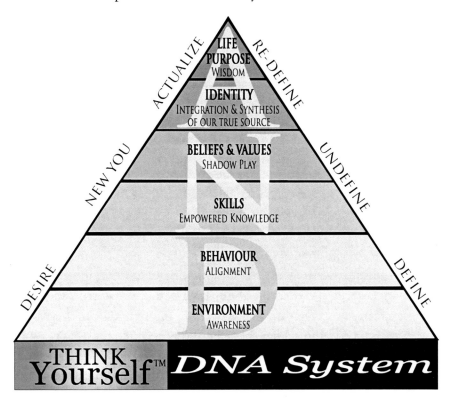

The pyramid of neurological levels is a great tool to help us better see who we are on the inside, which is often reflected in how we show up on the outside. The last decade of neuroscience research has discovered that our brains, previously assumed to be rigid and unchanging, are actually quite malleable, and in fact, receptive to change.

So what does that mean for you? It means that, with greater awareness and understanding of how you are 'wired', coupled with consistent and repeated effort, you can, in fact, 'change your stars' and 'change your fate!' You are not just the sum of all of your parts. You can choose to reorganize your bits and pieces and reinvent a much larger and more successful version of yourself.

We will be explaining each of the levels through the combined lens of Robert Dilt's Neurological Levels and Tasha Hughes six levels of her Diva Defence program. Dilt's title of each level is in bold and Tasha's is shadowed beneath.

LEVEL ONE ENVIRONMENT
AWARENESS 'I LIVE HERE'.

> *"You are the books you read, the movies you watch, the music you listen to, the people you spend time with, the conversations you engage in. Choose wisely what you feed your mind."* — *Unknown*

The Environment is where we live, play, work, and our surroundings. It is the places we go and the people with whom we interact.   In the animal world, it would be 'the habitat'. In the materialistic world, people often try to identify themselves by the type of car they drive, the neighbourhood in which they, the type of office they have. None of these actually represent who we really are on the inside. It is just part of our environment. Becoming identified with our environment can be very positive if the environment supports us in a healthy way. Sometimes we can become over-identified with our environment, or place the wrong importance on the environment, which does not support us in a healthy way.

As an example of looking into environment to fix a client's problem, you can refer to the woman Nathalie coached who was working in Saudi Arabia. She had an environmental problem. She wanted to move to a different country and relocate her humanitarian work. At first, she thought she needed to go back to school and work on her skills so she could get a different kind of job, but when she tuned into her values and beliefs, she was doing exactly the job she wanted. Her everyday life behaviours were great and she felt she could be herself. The problem was her environment. She needed to do exactly the same thing, but in a different environment. She has now moved to Germany and is happily pursuing her career in the same field, in a totally new setting.

Level One is also about Awareness, awareness of our boundaries, where do I end, where does someone else begin? Tasha often uses the yoga mat as an analogy for our environment. Becoming aware of the influences we allow into our lives (or onto our mats) is a healthy exploration towards our best success. Sometimes the things we allow in our environment offer clues to how we feel about ourselves, both positively and negatively. This awareness is crucial and foundational to our success in every way.

> *"What we consume is what we become."*   — *Tasha Hughes*

If our environment supports us, we can start to embrace our own unique strengths. We can unravel and disengage from impairments to our growth and success. Sometimes we realize we have placed the wrong people, wrong places and wrong situations in our environment, or maybe once they were very right, but no longer serve our forward movement.

Successful people surround themselves with an environment that supports that strong vision. Our success starts to become inevitable when we intentionally choose the right people, places and things, and build our vision from the ground up, (or in yoga, from the feet up).

LEVEL TWO BEHAVIOUR
ALIGNMENT / 'I ACT – REACT'

> *"Behaviour: The way in which we act or conduct ourselves, especially towards others. The way we respond to a particular situation or stimulus."*   — *Oxford Dictionaries*

Our behaviour is how we interact with family, friends and co-workers. It is what an observer may see, hear or feel when watching us engaged in a particular activity. Sometimes our behaviour can vary, depending upon our circumstances. When we feel confident and comfortable, our behaviour will reflect that. If we feel unsure, threatened or nervous, our behaviour reflects that as well.

Sometimes our behaviour is consistent with the success we say we want, and other times it is not. When it is not, it is often because change needs to happen at a different level. Implementing a 'success strategy' won't be effective if the problem lies at the level of 'Beliefs and Values' or 'Identity'

However, most of the time, the problem is in the values or beliefs layer and cannot be fixed at the behavioural level. If a problem resides in the identity or the belief system of a person, that is where the problem needs to be addressed. This explains why some of the past attempts at success failed. It is because it was not addressed at the right level. If you believe you are a failure —beliefs and values level — then doing a course on marketing or learning how to use Twitter - both behaviours—will not fix the problem. You will keep self-sabotaging yourself until you correct the beliefs.

Sometimes it is about disengaging from an old habit or way of being in the world, and consciously choosing to adopt new choices that are in alignment with your projected goal.

Each day and every hour we have the opportunity to stop, reflect and ask: "is this choice consistent with my bigger vision? Will this choice bring me closer or further away from my goal?"

When our minds and habits are out of alignment with our dreams of success, it is like trying to hang a beautiful yoga posture on a posturally-compromised body. It doesn't fit well, and certainly is not sustainable. The problem is one of alignment. If my body is not in alignment, I cannot create a strong pose. If my behaviour is out of alignment with dreams of success, I cannot create a strong present and future reality.

Much of the time, the negative thoughts we have are not actually our own, but were put there by someone else. Sometimes those negative thoughts were hand-me-downs from a caring parent, sometimes they were the cruel words of someone who did not have our best interest at heart. In any case, the words of Ghandi are an appropriate affirmation:

"I will not let anyone walk through my mind with their dirty feet."

However, when we are in alignment, when we keep the dirty feet out of our minds, we fall into the flow and grace of Life. There is a sense of ease and we act and react, or behave, from a place of trust. Trust in ourselves will generate behaviour that others can also trust.

LEVEL THREE: CAPABILITIES AND SKILLS
EMPOWERED KNOWLEDGE / 'I DO'

"Optimism is the faith that leads to achievement."   — *Helen Keller*

Capability represents our skills, what we're good at and whether or not we have innate capabilities and/or learned skills for dealing appropriately with an issue. We are not necessarily born with skills. We develop them as we age with our life experiences. When we use our skills and do what we are good at, we more likely feel in harmony with ourselves. When using our skills, we avoid that sense of wasting our talent. You have likely heard the saying: "Choose a job you love and you will never have to work a day in your life". In this context, it makes total sense. When we are good at something, we more likely love doing it. And we love doing more of it.

What are you really good at? What are the things that are very easy for you to do without even thinking about them? What made you decide to buy this book? It's awesome that you have it in your hands and you believe that there's something here that can help you. You gave yourself that motivation. You gave that to yourself because subconsciously, you knew you were ready for the next level. Your skills give you confidence and strength.

When you feel capable and skillful, you also feel knowledgeable. This leads to a greater state of empowerment. At this level, we experience greater confidence, proficiency and self-assuredness. We can begin to refine and pursue more complex plans or ideas.

Tasha says that Empowered Knowledge is marked by a renewed or newly discovered TRUST in ourselves and HOPE that positive change is within our grasp. It is a leap in our growth, marked by *vitality, energy and courage.* When we 'live' more authentically in the first two levels, it is reflected in the life choices we make. By releasing environments and behaviours that no longer serve us, and replacing them with those that do, we experience a release of vital energy to pursue our goals and dreams with more clarity and a renewed sense of possibility. With hope and trust come greater FREEDOM AND INDEPENDENCE.

When you actively choose what you allow onto 'your mat', (environment + behaviour), you create stronger boundaries. You learn how to become more skillful at that, and in doing so, you send a strong signal that you feel ready and capable of doing more.

At one point, Nathalie was coaching a female police officer. She wanted to change her unit and to move up to a different level in the force. She had tried before, unsuccessfully. She had even moved to a new city in order to apply in a different township, thinking she might have a better chance. It turned out that she had a skills problem. She was trying to fix it by changing her environment—moving to a different city—when in fact, she needed to take a few courses to upgrade her skills. She was convinced that she was capable of doing it, she had the proper beliefs and values to achieve her goal, so the problem was really a skill problem. Again, identifying where the problem resides is key to fixing it. She did take the crucial skill course and was able to apply for a higher ranked position within the same division. She is now managing the Evidence

Department and feels totally fulfilled by her work. She loves her job again!

LEVEL FOUR BELIEFS AND VALUES
SHADOW PLAY / 'I BELIEVE AND/OR I FEAR'

> *"Our deepest fear is not that we are inadequate. Our deepest fear is that we are powerful beyond measure ... We ask ourselves, "Who am I to be brilliant? Gorgeous? Talented? Fabulous?" Actually, who are you NOT to be? ... Your playing small does not serve the world... There is nothing enlightened about shrinking so that other people won't feel insecure around you. We are meant to shine."* — Marianne Williamson

Whether we believe something is possible or impossible, whether we believe it is necessary or unnecessary, whether or not we feel motivated about something is all driven by what is imprinted in our subconscious. This level is critical. What you believe is true, in your own representational systems, is forming who you are. Beliefs are at the base of our habits (good or bad). They are the main focus in the NEW YOU section of the System. We need to change our old negative beliefs in order to replace them with beliefs that will serve us better.

Personal work done at Levels One and Two, although sometimes intense with emotional content, are overall empowering and enlightening. Level Three embodies the tremendous learning of the first two levels and manifests as greater confidence, vitality and forward movement.

Following such tremendous gains, Level Four is both where deeper issues of the subconscious will arise AND the most primal of our survival instincts will be called upon. This is not easy!

Shadow Play is an invitation to 'sit with' those deeper fears of the subconscious, stopping to pause and all you can do is breathe through it. The amygdala (the reptilian part of our brain) gets triggered and screams 'Danger, Danger' as we start to move well beyond our previous comfort zones.

Patterns of self-sabotage at a much deeper level often show up after the gains of navigating more control of the first three levels.

You will know you have stepped into the sticky realm of Level Four if you find yourself saying, "I just keep doing THAT THING I said I wasn't going to do." Your choices defy logic as your subconscious mind rules, and the subconscious mind is often governed by fear.

We have given you some examples where some clients had environment, behaviour, or skill problems. These three are not the most common. Most people's problems reside in the beliefs, values and identity levels. The closer to the base of the pyramid, the easier it is to fix. You run out of milk, you go buy some. The closer to the identity level at the top, the more you see it as a real problem. An easy example of this is when someone has a self-confidence problem (belief) and to give themselves some more prestige and power, they buy themselves an expensive sports car. The problem is in the belief level (self-confidence) and they are trying to fix it in the environment level (sports car). It can't work. Again, the problem needs to be addressed where it belongs.

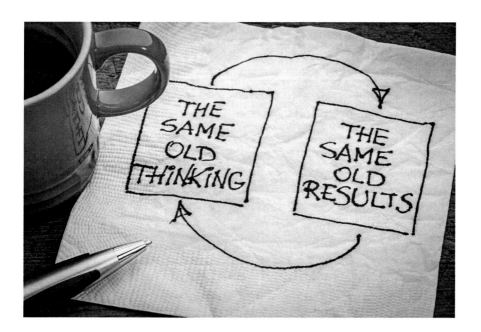

Our beliefs and values are guiding all our actions. When they make us grow and give us fulfilling lives, we can thank them for making life easy for us. When, on the other hand, they make us see the world from a negative angle, we wish we could change them. The beliefs that are not serving us are called limiting beliefs.

BEING SUCCESSFUL IS HARD. Says who? What if you chose to believe that it was easy? More likely, if you believe that being successful is hard, then you are telling your brain and programming it to make it difficult for you. Every time you think about this statement, or every time you say it out loud, you are giving a reason for your brain to make it hard for you.

WHEN YOU START MAKING MORE MONEY, YOU SPEND MORE, AND YOU ALWAYS STAY IN A POSITION WHERE YOU LIVE PAYCHECK TO PAYCHECK. This belief is not serving you either. The whole idea behind mind shifting is not to make you live on a tight budget or to teach you how to be wise with your money. This belief should be transformed into a belief that you will always have everything you need and that money will always show up.

IN MY FAMILY, WE WERE TOLD THAT WORKING IS BORING BUT WE ALL NEED A JOB. Really? Have you ever met someone who loves what they do? If it is possible for one person, it is possible for you. The whole science of this book is based on modeling. You can choose to model your parents or you can choose to model your successful friends or anyone who feels comfortable with their line of work.

THAT IS HOW I AM; I AM DOOMED TO STAY THIS WAY. We all have character and excel at our own skills . What can you dream, then? What if you want to be more of this or less of that? You can visualize yourself being the best of you. Any skill can be learned and any behaviour can be adopted.

NO MATTER HOW HARD I WORK OR WHAT I DO, I CAN'T GET ON TOP OF THINGS. Nothing ever worked? Ever? What would happen if it did? Have you ever thought that this belief, and its constant repetition in your head, might be the main reason that has kept you from getting on top of things all these years.

I DON'T HAVE WILLPOWER SO I CAN'T SUCCEED. How does not having willpower cause you to choose to believe that you can't succeed? Are these things even connected? Could willpower be an invention that we use as an excuse for our wrong programming?

I CANNOT LIVE WITHOUT MY TV SHOWS. Okay, we tend to agree with this. That is totally true! Just kidding. What would happen if you did live without them? Can you choose one or two? What if they fit into your downtime schedule? Being successful doesn't mean you're working 24/7. When specifically do you decide that it is time for TV? What if we could re-wire your brain to have a different *want* at this exact moment?

BEING SUCCESSFUL IS A LOT OF WORK. And being unsuccessful is not a lot of work? How about the hours you spent trying to fix problems that occurred because of your past failure?

PLANNING IS HARD AND GIVES ME HEADACHES. Every type of planning is hard? What if it could be fun? How would it be if you enjoyed it? Planning an exciting vacation abroad, for example. How about the first time you tried walking as an infant and fell. Thank goodness you kept trying and realized that walking is actually quite easy and doesn't hurt.

I HAVE CHILDREN SO I CANNOT BE SUCCESSFUL. Really? How many people do you know who are successful and do have children? What would happen if you stopped seeing children as a barrier? What if they could be your allies? Or your drive to succeed...

If you believe any of these beliefs, then that's what will happen to you. Remember, whether you believe you can do it or not, you are right either way.

"Believe you can and you're halfway there." — *Theodore Roosevelt*

LEVEL FIVE: IDENTITY
INTEGRATION & SYNTHESIS 'I AM'

"I AM currently under construction. Thank you for your patience."
— *Unknown*

The identity is who we are. Our self-esteem, our sense of self and what we identify with. This can include identifying with our job, marriage, religion, etc. It can also include how we interpret events in terms of our own self-worth. What we think we deserve or not.

You may be familiar with the expression, 'I AM a morning person.' This is a deep belief about who we are at a core level. We are not born to be morning or evening people. We choose to be more effective in the morning (or not) because we think so, act so and articulate this 'fact' to others. Saying the words: 'I AM' a morning person is a symbol of a deeply ingrained belief. It is much different from saying, "I work well in the morning" or "I get up early" which are behavioural affirmations and not identity-related.

Understanding each level of our own self and identifying where the problems lie is a great step towards fixing it. When I hear people say, "I am a fraud," it's important to know that the words I AM are very powerful. This means they don't only think of themselves as having unsuccessful attempts at success, they say I AM, which refers to their deeply ingrained beliefs at the level of their identity.

When we implement change, the higher we go on the neurological pyramid, the deeper we need to dig into our ingrained beliefs about ourselves in order to make the change. By changing cars or clothes, we are only changing an environmental aspect of our life. But by changing who we are, we lose, in some aspect, a portion of who we are.

Most people are quite wary of change, as no one wants to lose their own sense of self. Who are they going to be if they cannot be who they thought they were all their life? That is when re-writing our software and deciding what and who we want to be is an empowering tool that allows us to let go of our old self and embrace our new identity.

"All that we are is the result of what we have thought."   — *Buddha*

In Level Five, the new identity has been embraced. After facing all of the fears and contradictions layered into the first 4 layers, we can relax and celebrate in a place of integration and synthesis. There is less of a tendency to give our power away in exchange for external validation or to subvert our true identity for someone else's comfort.

In Tasha's *Diva Defence programme,* Level 5 is almost a return to innocence, as we can shift back to a state of play, fun and a new zest for life. The integrated 'I AM' is accompanied by a second bout of freedom. The first was experienced after Level 3, which we said was a renewed sense of trust in oneself, hope that positive change was possible, and a newly found sense of independence and freedom.

At this level of integration, our 'I AMs' are based on internal, not external validation. Freedom happens here as we discover that our true source is not our environment or other people, or limiting and self-sabotaging beliefs. When once we may have given our power away to another person, or a job, or a role, or our social identity as the source of our happiness, we now know that our 'I AMs' are much bigger.

Whenever we say to ourself: "I Am" we are referring to the Identity level, down in our deepest structure. However, before we got to our deepest self, our identity, it did start at a lower level of consciousness.

LEVEL SIX: LIFE PURPOSE
WISDOM / 'I KNOW' (AND I KNOW WHY)

"The meaning of Life is to find your gift. The purpose of life is to give it away." — *Pablo Picasso*

When all the layers of the pyramid are aligned and we live in a wanted environment, doing what we are good at and following our beliefs and values, then we can really feel like we are being who we are and living our real life purpose.

Our life purpose is the reason why we were put on this earth. Who else are you serving? What is beyond yourself? Who else are you serving with your life? What cause is close to your heart?

We can use the model to recognize how the various levels interact and how they are related. And it provides a means of recognizing at which level a problem is occurring and recognizing the most appropriate level at which to target the solution.

Here is one last example: Nathalie was coaching a businessman client who wanted to advance his career. One of his fundamental values is family. One of his complaints about work is that he has to work late. He's annoyed that he misses out on seeing his kids. He also holds a competitive trait as a fundamental value. So both of these values had to be addressed. He is a businessperson and he is a father. A happy person is a person who does what their highest purpose in life is and uses their skills following their beliefs and values. It's important to understand where you are on this spectrum and how to tweak your life to work with each of these. We realized that his family was more important to him than his career. So subconsciously, he was 'sabotaging' his possibilities of advancing in the company because he knew (again subconsciously) that it would mean seeing less of his kids. We then figured how to consciously satisfy his competitive desires while remaining on track with his family values. He is now happier at work where he has set some boundaries and works hard while he is there but is not staying after hours every day to satisfy his competitive nature. Instead, he has signed up for a hockey team and plays with friends twice a week, which satisfies his competitive thirst and also keeps him fit.

Level Six opens the door to a greater sense of Self-Mastery, which is almost always followed by leadership. At this point, there is no reason to compete with others (only ourselves). We can celebrate our own unique gifts as well as those of others. We can also recognize that there is a unifying oneness between us all.

Previous levels were marked by Knowledge and Hope. In Level Six, Knowledge translates into Wisdom and Hope turns into Faith. This level truly represents choice.

In Level Six, we understand that we are co-creators and co-conspirators in this game called Life. You know why you are here, what you are here to do, who you are here to serve (always a by-product of why + wisdom) and you live from your Life's Purpose.

Your decisions are based in wisdom. People are naturally drawn to you as a leader, because you are living your Why with a strong sense of conviction. That inspires confidence, trust and safety. People want to be around you because your success emanates from a deep place within yourself. You are unwavering and uncompromising in your purpose and commitment to living from a place of authenticity.

> *"Step out of the history that is holding you back. Step into the new story that you are willing to create."*   — *Oprah Winfrey*

KEY CONCEPTS:

THE FOUNDATION OF THE THINK YOURSELF™ D.N.A. SYSTEM

Our brain classifies information into different levels in the brain.

Environment. behaviours. Skill. Beliefs and Values. Identity. Life Purpose.

We need to identify where the problems are and fix them where they originate.

Beliefs and Values along with Identity are the main areas where the deeper problems reside.

Going through each layer will take you on a journey to define, un-define and re-define yourself.

PART 5:
THE "D"

CHAPTER 14

DESIRE - DEFINE

"The first principle of success is desire—knowing what you want. Desire is the planting of your seed." —Robert Collier

The first part of the D.N.A. System is DESIRE. This section revolves around the first two neurological levels: Environment and Behaviour.

You will discover your own character traits. You will fill out our very own personality test, discovering your Style-LIST, your superpower, your priorities, you fears, your possibilities for improvement, what drives you and motivates you. By discovering who you are, you will be able to define what you want. You have discovered already the characteristics of successful people. In light of your own profile, you will be able to determine which characteristics you want to add to your arsenal.

You will become aware of your current situation, what surrounds you and what physical evidence you will want to happen when you reach your goal. You will start aligning what you do in your everyday behaviours with what you 'should' do instead.

You will define what is success for you. You will be asked a multitude of questions with the intention of generating ideas in your brain that will allow you to elicit your perfect outcome and write your daily affirmation. This will serve as a reference, a plan, a map, a vision of your positive outcome.

In the DESIRE part, you will also learn how the 'don'ts' in your language have been wired in your brain. You will understand that the brain is at the base of your actions as the mind and body are connected. You will understand another reason why your old techniques did not work because they were temporary, as opposed to being built-in, like a definitive new habit.

Finally, this section will invite you to dare, eliciting exactly what you want, aiming for a plethora of choices and opportunities, and following the real intent behind your desires.

Enjoy the process, discovering yourself and what you really want.

KEY CONCEPTS

DESIRE DEFINE

The first part of the D.N.A System is DESIRE. This section of the book will help you define who you are and what you want.

CHAPTER 15

THE STYLE-LIST TEST
WHO AM I?

"The women whom I love and admire for their strength and grace did not get that way because shit worked out. They got that way because shit went wrong, and they handled it. In a thousand different ways on a thousand different days, but they handled it." — *Elizabeth Gilbert*

Before you are able to define your desires and know what you want, it is necessary to know who you are. This section is offering you a tool that will help you discover and define who you are and then what drives you. We are simply helping you identify what style you are. It is important to point out that none of your characteristics are set in stone. This tool helps you understand your 'old-you' and gives you a clue about areas where you may want to focus on becoming more of. Ideally, you would find yourself in the sweet spot in the centre, owning multiple characteristics of each four styles of the Style-LIST test. Lots of people have one dominant style. For others, their results reveal that their two dominant styles are even or maybe the first three. The information you will discover is designed to guide you towards writing down your DESIRE and DEFINE yourself. Before you can place your order or write your software, it is interesting to know where you stand and what characteristics are suggested for you for which to aim.

When you fill out this Personality 'Style-LIST' self-assessment tool, remember on which area of the balance wheel you are working. Your answers will differ depending on the context in which you are placing yourself. Make sure you fill out all questions for the same context to ensure congruency with the results. For example, the answers for your personal life in your role as a wife or mother may be very different from what you would say about yourself in your professional life.

This self-assessment tool provides you with an easy and fun way to learn about your own personality style (comprised from a four quadrants Style-LIST profile) and help you identify the common Personality Types you most naturally interact and with which you have relationships.

Research on human emotions and behaviour dates as far back at 1893 when psychologist William Moulton Marston published his findings in a book titled 'Emotions of Normal People',in 1928. After that he contributed to the creation of the DISC assessment along with psychologist Walter Clarke who later constructed a modern day assessment model based on Moulton Marston's theories. While there are a variety of personality profile self-assessment tools available, we decided to create a fun and easy 'Style-LIST' self-assessment, adapted from a simplified version of the DISC. The self-assessment takes only minutes to complete and will help you learn more about yourself, others, and how you naturally behave in situations where interpersonal emotions are a factor. It is important to know that while your profile is based on a blend of four primary personality styles, we will help you identify your primary and secondary styles for the purposes of self-discovery.

> *Fun FACT*
>
> *Here is interesting information on the DISC personality test. The designer of the original DISC profile also created the comic 'Wonder Woman'.*

Marston, William M. (1928). Emotions of Normal People. K. Paul, Trench, Truber & Co. ltd,

Knowing your own profile and dominating style will help you better understand why it is that you interact with some people easier than others. Having this insight into personality profiles will also help you tailor your communication style and even your behaviour with those you identify, with a different Personality profile then yourself. The most important thing to know is that by knowing more about yourself and your natural personality profile (within the role in which you are choosing to evaluate yourself), you will be more successful in relating to and adapting your approach based upon those you interact and work with or with whom you have a personal relationship.

Do not judge that one style is better than another. Also you must know that your profile will change based on the environment (and role) you are in. We recommend you take this self-assessment based on the role you are most interested in focusing on with this book. Take the assessment for other roles too. Typically you will find your dominant and secondary personality style may either flip order or your style will change altogether (where your lower scores become higher and vice versa). Also by knowing yourself better you can build on your own Personality style and as you begin to recognize others' styles, you can adapt your style to positively influence your interactions with others. A couple of interesting insights into human emotions and behaviour: almost fifty percent of all people exhibit behaviour combining three of the four styles (all three scores are close) and these people tend to be more flexible and adaptable than others. Fifty percent of all people exhibit behaviour combining two styles and only a very small percent of people exhibit behaviour primarily from one style. Therefore we should not 'stereotype' anyone.

The combination of all four styles constitutes your behaviour or the way you illustrate your personality that is unique to you: L—Leader, I—Influencer, S—Supporter, T—Thinker.

When you take the assessment, think about the average day you have had over the last six months, in the role in which you are 'THINKING Yourself™ SUCCESSFUL'. Reflect upon, replay in your mind, and visualize the average conversations, interactions, thoughts and behaviour you exhibited in two types of scenarios; one which was highly successful and one in which you experienced challenge or conflict. This will help you 'get into character' to evaluate your emotional responses to the questions.

The best use of this self-assessment tool is to learn more about yourself, others and how to deal in situations where interpersonal relationships are involved.

In our version of DISC, the model is represented with four Styles-LISTs where each style will be given a full chapter. You will first take the test to identify your primary and secondary style, then you will be able to consult each chapter to see what your main characteristics are, what drives you, and what could be your fears and opportunities to grow. We will also give you some tips on how to communicate with someone of that specific style. You may even discover, as you will read the other profile as well (not just your two major ones), that there are some characteristics in your less prominent styles that you may want to acquire and program into your "future-you".

TAKE THE Style-LIST TEST

Instructions:

1. You will rank each question's response with a number on a scale from 1 to 4 as follow:

   1 = least like you

   2 = rarely like you

   3 = occasionally like you

   4 = most like you

2. You may use each number only once per question.

3. When you have answered all of the questions, you will total the numbers respective to each quadrant and enter that total in the appropriate box at the end of the quiz.

4. Record your highest score on the line beside 'Primary Style-LIST' and your second highest score on the line beside 'Secondary Style-LIST'"

Example: Your ideal vacation would be ...

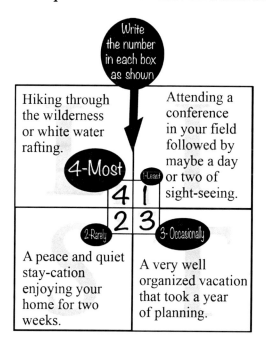

QUESTIONS

Question 1.
When working with a group on a project ...

You think people should do what you say because your ideas are best.	You are eager to work with the team and can't wait to get started!
You will let someone else get the ball rolling and see where the project goes.	You like to make sure everything is done just right before handing it in.

Question 2.
In the best conversations you have ...

Your conversations are brief and to the point. You can say everything with the least amount of words.	You get to talk a lot and laugh often. The conversation feels friendly, fun and open.
You are an excellent active listener and let the others say all that they have to say before making your comment.	You feel like you say everything you want to say clearly and precisely.

Question 3.
Your life motto would be …

"Take every chance, drop every fear."	"Believe you can and you will."
"We are stronger together than we are alone."	"You can find anything, if you know how to look hard enough."

Question 4.
When out for dinner with friends and it is time to order …

You decide on your entrée and then tell your friends to have the same item because you know it will be really good.	You wait until the server comes to you and then go with the first thing you see.
As a group, you collectively decide on a couple of appetizers to share.	You don't have to worry about it you order the same item every time because you know you will like it.

Question 5.
When facing a challenging task, you would …

Be confident in your abilities to tackle any problem and tackle the problem head on.	Dive in and use your instincts to go in the direction that feels right in the moment.
Ask others what they think you should do to maximize your skills and those of others.	Explore the issue from every angle and understand as much as you can, then take action.

Question 6.
Your ideal vacation would be …

Hiking through the wilderness or white water rafting.	Attending a conference in your field followed by maybe a day or two of sight-seeing.
A peace and quiet stay-cation enjoying your home for two weeks.	A very well organized vacation that took a year of planning.

Question 7.
In relationships …

You are confident meeting new people and initiating conversations with others.	You love making new friends and you find it easy to trust people.
You have only a few close friends and you always do everything together.	You are very respectful of your friendships and are always kind to each other. You understand the importance of giving each other space when needed.

Question 8.
If you could choose your legacy from the following, it would be …

To be one of the first humans in history to set foot on Mars.	To inspire others to reach their full potential in ways such as writing a book or becoming a motivational speaker.
To be happy and content with who you are inside.	To find a solution to the problem of climate change.

Question 9.
If you had to choose you would go to the following group fitness class …

A program with a clear focus, such as lifting weights, where you feel like you are accomplishing something and getting stronger.	A high-energy cardio or dance based class where you can move around and have fun with your friends.
A yoga class where you can relax and just be.	A group cycling class where you feel you can ride at your own pace and stay in control of your workout.

Question 10.
In your place of work, it is most important that …

Your company maintain its status and gain recognition as leaders in your industry.	Everyone gets along and have a good time while doing your jobs.
You feel safe and comfortable about where you work and understand what is expected of you.	You are always looking for ways to improve and finding new innovations to make your company stronger.

Total Score.
Add up the score for each style and
enter your totals in the boxes below.

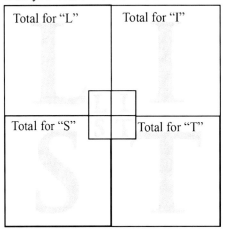

Total for "L"	Total for "I"
Total for "S"	Total for "T"

PRIMARY Style-LIST (Highest score): _____

SECONDARY Style-LIST (2nd highest score): _____

Are you a Leader, an Influencer, a Supporter or a Thinker? Are you a
blend of all of them (are your numbers really close to each other)? Is
there one dramatically higher than the others? Is your lowest one off
by two or by ten? Is there a big gap between your top and your lowest?
Everybody is different. The study shows that we are all a blend of all
four styles.

Now that you have determined your Style-LIST personality (primary
and secondary), let's discover the characteristics for each of the
Style-LIST.

KEY CONCEPTS

1. The best use of this Personality Profile self-assessment is to learn more about yourself, others and how to understand how and why people interact the way that they do.

2. Half of the population exhibits behaviour representing at least 2 or 3, and even all 4 of the styles and only a small percentage (5%) of the population exhibit behaviour from only one style LIST.

3. Do not stereotype anyone. Use this self-assessment Personality Profile to gain insight and understanding or as a tool to adapt your style when interacting with people that you may identify as different than you.

CHAPTER 16

LEADER

"Well-behaved women rarely make history." — *Laurel Thatcher Ulrich*

People with a Leader's dominant style like to be in charge. Being commander is part of their highest priorities. They are pioneers in their thinking and their behaviours. They are the first ones to acquire new methods, new technology, the latest and the greatest systems. They are definite, determined and dominating. You will often see them leading the pack.

A Leader is motivated by power and authority. They will work hard to get a title, a prize, a special recognition or a perk that only the top achievers can get. They are attracted by the VIP special privileges that come with their achievement. They are very competitive and they love winning. They compare themselves to others and they get a high when overcoming challenges. Reaching targets, getting results and success in general is at the base of their inner-self, driving them to keep going higher and higher.

A leader's strengths include high self-confidence and high ego. They believe in their capacities, and are willing to take risks, be bold and assertive in order to continually perform and feed their own confidence.

They fear losing their power and control. They could be what we often call 'a control-freak' . They don't like being taken advantage of and being perceived as vulnerable. You will rarely see a Leader when they are not at their best. They usually retreat back to avoid being witnessed when they don't feel they will portrait a strong and confident image.

When a Leader is over extended they may become impatient, insensitive and show lack of concern.

A natural Leader should be aware of certain areas with potential for improvement. They may want to slow down or give some time as they may be too fast paced (impatient). They may be too blunt or abrupt, as in a Leader's model of reality, time and ultimate goals matter more than the emotions of the people in front of them. Leaders may say exactly what is on their mind. They may intimidate or create fear in others. Others can see them as being too insensitive.

> *"I've worked very hard at understanding myself, learning to be asser-*
> *tive. I'm past the point where I worry about people liking me."*
> — *Pam Dawber*

If you have recognized this type in some of your entourage, you may want to read carefully how to handle them in your life. To communicate with a dominant Leader, you want to be direct, brief and to the point.

Unlike other styles, the Leader won't enjoy having a conversation about their personal life, their kids, etc. They want to go straight to the point. Be efficient. Reflect on the facts and focus on the task. Stick to business or the point and have a results-oriented approach. Identify opportunities or challenges to peak their interest and provide a win-win situation. Use a logical approach, touching on key points and do not over-do details. Compliment a Leader and appear confident yourself.

To best work with a dominant Leader, create momentum (action), competition and challenge them with new goals/opportunities to achieve. Utilize the newest and quickest techniques and methods to achieve. Acknowledge performance gains and efforts.

The percentage of the population that displays a dominant Leader style as their primary style is 10 percent.

KEY CONCEPTS

LEADER

A leader is naturally dominant and confident, action- focused and motivated by challenge, competition.

While only a small percentage of the population are naturally dominant Leaders they are movers and shakers.

CHAPTER 17

INFLUENCER

"Think twice before you speak, because your words and influence will plant the seed of either success or failure in the mind of another."
— *Napoleon Hill*

The Influencer is the Social Butterfly of the styles. Just watch them work a room or gather the co-operation of others towards a common goal. Influencers have the ability to rally the troops. Often highly intuitive and sensitive to the moods and body language of those around them, when harnessed, this gift can assist them in unifying unexpected camps. Often high energy, Influencers have a keen sense of humour used to sway people to see their vision, and encourage camaraderie and goodwill.

Influencers are often planners, but not implementers. They tend to be idea-incubators with big start-up energy, leaving the implementation to Supporters and/or Thinkers. Natural networkers, Influencers can sweep others into the wave of their ideas with charisma and magnetism. Influencers inspire collaboration.

> *"I'd rather regret the things I have done, than regret the things I have not done."* — *Lucille Ball*

The Influencer's priorities include: being pioneering, energizing and encouraging. They want to be the first one to discover something and they go about telling the whole world about it. They are the one making you try this new product that they have found. They influence you to switch to the "new thing" or the "new way of doing something" in such a dynamic way that you can't resist. Their energy is contagious and they want to make sure everybody gets their share of their vitality.

An interactive Influencer is motivated by: social recognition, group activities and friendly relationships. They apply to contests, they like others to know about their latest and greatest. They want to be included. Belong. They thrive when with others and even at work, they make a point of supporting familiarity and amicable rapport with co-workers, clients, employees and superiors.

Their strengths include: optimism, talkativeness, enthusiasm, sociability (people-oriented) and charm. They are the half-full glass personification. They see the bright side of things and are eager to share their confident views of life with others. They are always "in" when asked to go to a social event - when they are not the one organizing it -, ready for another opportunity to get together and talk to people. They entertain the room wherever they go.

Their fears include: social rejection, disapproval, loss of influence and being ignored. They are afraid to be excluded from social opportunities - Fear Of Missing Out (FOMO) - and are concerned when people choose to follow someone else's idea. They would rather change their opinion quickly when talking about something than being disapproved of, and they are devastated if they get forgotten and not invited to an event.

When an Influencer is over extended they may become: disorganized, impulsive and have lack follow through.

Areas that an interactive Influencer should be aware of (with potential for improvement) include: may be too indirect when communicating, may speak before thinking, may be overly optimistic, may be disorganized, may be too overly trusting, may abandon when in conflict and may have difficulty completing tasks or follow through.

How to Communicate with an Influencer: allow time for socialization and interaction with people, ask for opinions and feelings, show caring and genuine interest and appreciation in the person, be friendly and non-threatening, involve them in the brainstorming of new ideas and approaches, expect quick decisions with less facts or statistics to back their decision and provide opportunities for recognition and reward and complement.

How to best work with an Influencer: recognize effort as often as you can, provide lots of variety and change, do not get too serious and be approachable, make it fun and let them talk.

The percentage of the population that displays an Influencer's style as their primary style is twenty percent.

KEY CONCEPTS

INFLUENCER

An interactive Influencer is highly social, enthusiastic and people-oriented and motivated by opportunity to pioneer new things.

While this Personality style only represents a small percentage of the population they light up a room with their presence.

CHAPTER 18

SUPPORTER

"The purpose of human life is to serve and to show compassion and the will to help others." — *Albert Schweitzer*

Supporters like to exist within the safety and familiarity of structured relationships and environment. Group-oriented, they create balance and harmony. They also honour traditions and prefer tried and true methods. Supporters feel the most freedom within the safety of established systems and boundaries. They are protective, adaptive and take pride in providing nurturance and nourishment.

A steady Supporter's priorities include: the need to serve others, being humble and inclusive. They will notice if someone is alone or in need and run to the rescue - if it is not themselves as they tend to be discreet and modest. They volunteer sometimes in multiple organizations. Look for Supporters in PTAs, church groups, social committees, volunteering, and in any other capacity where they are needed, helpful and appreciated.

A Supporter is motivated by: stable environments, traditional practices, sincere appreciation, cooperation, and opportunities to help others (people-oriented). They don't necessarily like change and they are comfortable in sameness and repetition. They are fantastic at following processes and methods and won't sway from protocol or from what has been done in the past.

Their strengths include: loyalty, patience, they are a team player and results-oriented, a good listener, have a calming approach and are modest. They are like a mother for everyone around. They take care of others, they are the go-to person when someone needs an ear or a pat on the back. They work well in a team and will support other people's idea before theirs in order to maintain harmony. They are loyal to their friends and are the friend that hasn't changed hairdresser in over twenty years. "If it's not broken, why change it?"

Their fears include: loss of stability, change, loss of harmony (status quo) and offending others. They don't like to be shaken out of their comfort zone. They are the politically correct and respectful friend that would rather keep something for themselves, than risking to offend you.

When they are over-extended they may become: possessive, may avoid change, be indecisive and over-accommodating.

Areas that a steady Supporter should be aware of (with potential for improvement) include: may be possessive, may be indirect, may tolerate too long before making a change, may be too adaptable, may be too low risk and may resist.

How to Communicate with Supporter: be patient, draw out their opinions and provide a logical approach to the facts. Relax and allow time for discussion and show how change or solutions will benefit them.

Quantify expectations, goals and rewards and involve them in the change plan and process, offer support and reward regularly.

How to best work with them: be consistent and limit change (step by step), progress slowly and steadily. Tell them about you and what you have learned and ask what they think about it. Involve them in the decision making and use a tried and proven, safe approach.

The percentage of the population that display a Supporter style as their primary style: sixty percent.

KEY CONCEPTS

SUPPORTER

A steady Supporter is loyal, patient, people oriented, a great listener and nurturer.

The largest percentage of the population are steady Supporters and they help maintain calm and carry on.

CHAPTER 19

THINKER

"I'd take precision any day over power; as far as being tactical you know you have to see what's going on in there and also understand that for every punch that you or your opponent throws there's always a counter shot or two which you have to be ready to fire or defend." —— *Alexis Arguello*

A cautious Thinker makes a priority of being accurate. They are deliberate and firm. The little detail is important. They will think of all angles and will have planned everything, having a plan B, C and D. They will hold their ground until they get all the details they need. The Thinker will work well with the 'big-picture', people who would be incapable of making things happen. The Thinker will take the vision and chunk it down into a step-by-step detailed plan in order to achieve the big picture.

They are motivated by opportunities to gain knowledge and to use their expertise. They love to learn and apply new concepts. They produce high quality work, very precise and perfect. They enjoy having critical discussions and complex problems to solve.

Their strengths include accuracy, precision, analysis and organization. When they tell a story they don't miss any detail and can stay organized in their thoughts. They love processes and classifications. Their desk, their home and their life reflects order and everything is in its place. Perfectly organized in a way that makes sense!

They fear criticism of their work. They will continue to perfect it until they are certain to avoid any critic. They don't like being wrong. They will argue and justify their thoughts or actions to prove that they were right, in their own way. They like to go through everything meticulously and every step of the process. They don't like taking short cuts.

> *"I'm never pleased with anything, I'm a perfectionist, it's part of who I am."* — *Michael Jackson*

When a cautious Thinker is over extended they may become overly critical. They may isolate themselves and have the tendency to over analyze.

The Thinker also has some areas with potential for improvement. They should be aware that they may require excessive data before coming to a decision. They may be too slow to act. They may be too critical, especially of themselves and may work too long to perfect projects before they can actually hand them in. They may be too low risk and may internalize feelings.

If you deal with Thinkers, you may be interested in knowing how to best communicate with them. Use data and facts. Be objective, examining arguments from all sides using a logical approach. Use words like: 'it makes sense', 'in light of this, thorough analysis", Keep on task with them. Do not socialize. If you disagree with them, disagree with the facts not the person. They don't like to be criticized. Do not invade their personal space. Focus on quality and stick to proven ideas, limiting 'new' ideas.

To best work with a cautious Thinker, provide reports and lots of details. Be well prepared and on time. Thinkers' biggest pet peeve is people arriving late or not prepared. Be structured, precise, accurate and stress high standards. Follow rules, policy and procedure and allow them to ask 'Why?'

The percentage of the population that displays a cautious Thinker as a primary style is fifteen percent.

KEY CONCEPTS

THINKER

A cautious Thinker desires accuracy, loves deliberate on facts, values accuracy and precision and being organized.

Although a small percentage of the population, cautious Thinkers keep the rest of the population organized and on time.

CHAPTER 20

WHAT DRIVES YOU

"Passion is energy. Feel the power that comes from focusing on what excites you." — *Oprah Winfrey*

Now that you have discovered your primary and secondary Style-LIST, you are aware of the behavioural traits or characteristics you already possess and those you want to add to your repertoire of tools for success.

We will now address one of the most common drivers of behaviour that successful women possess: Motivation. Scientists have identified different types of motivation or motives—physiological and social—and have discovered that social motives are specific only to human beings (while physiological motives are present in both animals and human beings). These are called social motives because they are learned and the strength of one type of social motive or another will vary from one individual to another, which explains why some people have greater levels of drive to succeed than others. With knowledge of social motives, we have the potential to learn how to harness motivation and take success to the next level.

Motivation, by its definition, is the desire to do things. To succeed at something you must have a motive or a deep desire. Motivation can also be described as the reason(s) one has for acting or behaving in a particular way. Other words for motivation are: drive, enthusiasm, ambition, initiative and determination. It's about figuring out what is important to you, and why, so that you know what you want and why, then having the desire to reach new levels of success.

Those who are wildly successful have heaps of motivation. While successful people may not always know what they are doing, they have a driving motive that is developed from an emotional state. They don't take no for an answer. When things get difficult, they push through and make things happen, negotiate or influence others as needed and do not quit until they achieve their goal(s) - that's what motivation is about.

While there are many types of social motivation, we have chosen to focus on the three main social motives that subconsciously drive your behaviour. Most people will identify with one motive more than the others. The key is to find out what motive fuels you the most and use it to your advantage! Before we do help you identify your primary motive, let's see where motivation comes from and how you access and utilize it to achieve success.

Motivation is regulated by a part of the brain called the nucleus accumbens. This is a small region of the brain that regulates the flow of neurotransmitters between the brain and different nerve cells in the body and strongly influences whether or not you have the desire do things like go to the gym, eat healthy and prospect new clients. One neurotransmitter worth mentioning is dopamine because it is this brain chemical released from this region of the brain that plays a major role in triggering motivation and reward-motivated behaviour. Dopamine also influences memory, cognition, sleep and mood. Behavioural neuroscientists and psychologists say that dopamine helps bridge the psychological gap between sitting on the couch thinking about exercising and getting off the couch and to the gym and actually exercising.

SOCIAL MOTIVES

Just as important as the hormonal and neurotransmitter factors that influence your motivation, there are three main social motives that drive your behaviour: Power, Affiliation and Achievement. Think of these unconscious motives like the gasoline that you put into your car's fuel tank to fuel your drive, even when the road to success becomes challenging.

Each of us is driven by all three to some extent, but most people identify with one more than the others. These social motives are what compel you to your goal, and if you do not use them, your emotional state will not be revved up enough (like putting your foot on the gas), your progress will be slower or you may not reach your goal at all.

It is important to know that dopamine spikes whenever something goes better than expected (when you exceed your goal) or when you receive an unexpected reward. Michael T Treadway, PhD at Department of Psychology at Emory University says that "When something feels better than expected, dopamine sends a signal to your brain that says "I need to figure out how to make it happen again." For example, you are asked to complete a challenging work assignment; one that will impact the overall success of the company and you know that you will have to influence decision makers of your ideas (that will require changes to policy). You have never worked directly with the level of management before however you complete the work and your proposal is unanimously accepted. You feel like 'wonder woman' having accomplished this difficult feat and you feel empowered to take on even more responsibility at work. That's dopamine working for you. Unfortunately, your brain will get used to that feeling quickly and after a few experiences you come to expect the same 'high'. Your dopamine levels will no longer spike quite as high and you will begin to feel less excited about difficult work tasks. In order to stay motivated you will have to raise the odds, turn up the difficulty of the challenge. To keep your motivation high and dopamine spiking take on new challenges (in pursuit of new goals) every few weeks or so. Those who exercise know that to keep motivation high they must also switch up their exercise routine every 4-6 weeks. "If nothing changes, then nothing changes." Maureen Hagan

POWER

People who are power motivated strive to exercise strong, influence action, generate strong emotions in others, are concerned about reputation or position in the world. They are usually successful mentors, trainers, teachers or instructors of others. They seek positions of leadership,

authority and status and they are most often the leaders within their company. They receive gratification from being in a leadership position. This social motive is often called 'influence motivation'.

> *"Power to me is the ability to make a change in a positive way."*
> — *Victoria Justice*

Nathalie is mainly driven by power. She has made her life purpose to inspire others to achieve being their best and to live a fulfilling life. Whenever challenges happen in her life, it is always the thought of those who look up to her that inspire her to keep going. "One year at a fitness expo where I had the chance to see my absolute idol Lisa Osborne, feeling like a kid or a groupie at a rock concert, cherishing the picture I had been able to take with my hero, I was standing in line to buy a new pair of runners at the expo when a lady came towards me in excitement and told her girlfriend: "That's her, that's Nathalie, OMG, please take a picture with my fitness instructor, she is so awesome!!!" So I turned around and looked behind her to whom this woman was referring. Then I realized it was me. Surprised, I smiled and let my 'fan' take a picture with me and ironically was thinking how weird it was that somehow, the very same experience I just had with my own idol was replicating itself a few minutes later. I thought: "tell her, I am really nobody, I am just a fitness instructor, but for this woman, I guess I am more than I thought I was. I always remember that moment in every action, reminding myself that whatever I do, someone is looking up and I must be my best to meet the expectations of my 'fans' and mainly my own expectations."

It is when we are not our best that causes us to be miserable or feel inadequate. It is not when we make mistakes or when we learn something we don't know. It is when we know better and we disappoint ourselves that we take it hard. Nathalie thrives when it involves people that are subject to be inspired, when someone is watching. When faced with a decision making process, she always asks herself the question: "What would someone who needs to be inspired, expect me to do here?"

AFFILIATION

People who are affiliation-motivated strive to establish, maintain and restore close relationships with others. They characterize group activities as social, friendly and collaborative. The need for being around and working cohesively with others while creating participation is key. They tend to be good therapists, consultants and supporters and they are most often effective in management roles that require relationship building.

Tasha is driven by Affiliation. Tasha was an only child, and an Introvert, who learned to adapt and masquerade as an Extrovert. While growing up, she traveled a lot with her parents for figure-skating and tennis events. She spent a LOT of time in hotel pools. Her stepfather, a former Canadian Figure-Skating Coach and International Judge (aka Big Bear) always told her she was brave, and encouraged her to make friends with the other kids on vacation, who likely were not as brave as she. "I spent a lot of time in daycare and at baby-sitters while my Mom was at work. As an only child, I also had an imagination, which was frequently referred to as 'wild', and a personality that was 'theatrical'. I discovered that laughing and story-telling were great ways to make friends. I figured out how to engage an entire group in imaginative play, so I didn't have to always play by myself. I also learned how to listen very well, both to what was and wasn't being said."

Today, Tasha is often referred to as a 'social butterfly', and is highly motivated to spend time with colleagues, friends and family at business events and social gatherings. Students often become friends, as she takes a special interest in their lives beyond the training. She LOVES people. She loves studying people. She is a connector. From her perspective, everyone has a story, and she wants to know what it is. She tends to see the beauty and goodness in people first, and is driven to bring that to the forefront.

Tasha thrives as a "cheerleader" and is motivated by gathering in, participating with, and leading a group. In terms of her professional life, the more the merrier. She feels a sense of accomplishment if her students feel 'seen', 'heard' and more powerful because of her work.

ACHIEVEMENT

The goal of achievement motivation is the need to outperform others, meet or beat self-imposed stretch goals or standards of excellence and, to strive for innovative and unique accomplishments. Achievement-motivated people enjoy setting and achieving challenging goals. They are successful entrepreneurs yet they may not be as effective in managerial roles because they are often too demanding. On the other hand they love competition.

When success is the goal, Mo is driven by achievement. She is very goal oriented, performs best when she is given deadlines to achieve, whether it is on her own or on a team. "I learned very early in life how to turn challenge into opportunity and use my birth order to lead. I fondly remember stories that my mother told me about my drive to thrive as a very premature twin and my competitive instincts to catch up with my twin sister, and my peers. In school I was not the most gifted when it came to academics, sport or theatre arts. However, my 'can-do', 'no-quit' attitude helped me to achieve many goals and much success later in life.

I enjoy tackling challenges to overcome the odds and get fired up when someone says something cannot be done. If told that it is impossible, I respond: "watch me!". Mo needs to have challenging but relevant goals with deadlines because that keeps her on point.

To really get to know which social motives drive you, you need to tap into your emotions to really see what drives your behaviour. Visualization is an effective way in which to tap. Think about a situation in which you are at the centre of attention, such as when you are giving a presentation. Focus on everything—from what you are wearing, what the room looks like and how many people are sitting in front of you in the audience. Then ask yourself 'how do I feel?' If you have a positive emotional response to this situation and you feel confident and strong, that is a sign you are driven by power. If you feel comfortable or somewhat anxious you are motivated by affiliation or achievement. If you were imagining how you could network with the people in your audience, your motive is affiliation. If you are driven by achievement, you envisioned getting over your fear of public speaking or imagined a standing ovation following your presentation, motivated by the opportunity to overcome your fear or nervousness of speaking in public. Which motive did you relate to the most in this scenario?

SELF-ASSESSMENT
WHAT IS YOUR DOMINATING SOCIAL MOTIVE?
WHAT TRIGGERS YOU AT AN EMOTIONAL LEVEL?

Ask yourself what triggers your motivation? What raises your level of dopamine? As you ask yourself the following four questions choose one answer that best represents your primary motive. Choose either a, b or c.

1. How do you go about social media?

a) *You first look at your own posts and get a rush when you see the number of likes on your own post going up.*

b) *You mostly look at other people's posts and would spend most of your time commenting on others versus promoting yourself.*

c) *You look at other people's post and compare yours with theirs, secretly competing (keeping score) with their number of 'shares', 'views' or 'likes' with your own.*

2. Your girlfriend invited you to her gym to try a spinning class. What was your experience like?

a) *While it was your first class, you found it easy to keep up and excel. You looked like a pro and even others commented about your level of skill.*

b) *You enjoyed the group fitness experience because of the new friends you made in the class and look forward to seeing them along with your girlfriend again.*

c) *You felt an adrenalin rush especially from the competitiveness of the class and can't wait to experience that winning feeling again.*

3. Your boss tells you that he needs you to take on a difficult project with a tight deadline, how do you react?

a) *You feel empowered and immediately take action on your own, take responsibility to lead the project and influence others to help you.*

b) *You consider who you would like to reach out to, to help accomplish this project and seek others input and creative ideas.*

c) *You look forward to the challenge, knowing that while it won't be easy you are determined to make it happen.*

4. You decide to go on vacation with your two best girlfriends. How will you go about choosing a destination?

a) *You know in your mind where you and your friends should go and you take initiative to find the 'perfect' destination and use your influence to convince them.*

b) *You are happy to go where your girlfriends decide because you are just happy to be vacationing with your friends.*

c) *You suggest a 'friendly' competition in which the winner gets to choose the destination.*

5. You are on the re-decorating committee at the office.

a) *You have a brilliant idea about what it should look like. You bring everyone on board with your suggestion and work hard at making it absolutely amazing so that others will look up to you.*

b) *You make sure that everyone's opinion is heard and you help in allowing your co-workers to all pitch in with their ideas. Ultimately, you will lean towards what the majority likes so that as many people as possible will be happy with the final choice.*

c) *You get a rush from preparing material before the meeting so that you will be the first one with concrete suggestions.*

6. You are watching your child's team play soccer. Which player do you notice the most, or who do you want your child to be?

a) *The 'alpha' player who plays their position well, and can tell the other players how to play theirs as well.*

b) *The child who congratulates another player for a great play, or encourages them when they make a mistake?*

c) *The striker who gets a hat-trick in many of the games?*

7. You have planned a personal shopping day.

a) *You plan to go shopping on your own; you prefer it that way so that you can 'power shop' and keep to your own schedule and shop only the stores that interest you. You are on a mission to find the hottest dress for an upcoming event at work and you want to stand out wearing something spectacular (and that no one else is wearing).*

b) *You have invited your girlfriends along so that together you can find the perfect dress for your upcoming event. You enjoy and seek out the opinions of your friends when it comes to buying clothes for yourself.*

c) *You wait until the week before your special event to shop for that perfect dress. You are confident that you will find something amazing last minute, and you enjoy the challenge of shopping last minute. In fact you set it as a goal to find the hottest dress in the least amount of time.*

If you answered mostly a), your strongest emotional motive is Power. If you mostly answered b), your strongest emotional motive is Affiliation. If you mostly answered c), your strongest emotional motive is Achievement.

YOUR PRIMARY MOTIVE: _____

Once you know what motive(s) drive you, then, refer to that knowledge when you look for ways and strategies to help you raise those motive(s) to fuel you to reach your goals.

KEY CONCEPTS

SOCIAL MOTIVES

The three main social motives are Power, Affiliation and Achievement.

Those who succeed have learned how to tap into their social motives and leverage this chemical 'super-power'. Those who succeed are high achievers.

CHAPTER 21

WHAT DO YOU WANT?

"Decide what you want, decide what you are willing to exchange for it. Establish your priorities and go to work." — H. L. Hunt

Now that you know your personality profile and what drives you, you can now start deciding what you want. Whether your Style-LIST is closer to the Leader or the Influencer or the Supporter or the Thinker, and whether you are presently driven by power, affiliation or achievement, everything is temporary and you are now taking charge of what and who you want to be.

The next few chapters will help you create a compelling image of yourself achieving your goal.

After embracing the questions we will offer you, there can be holes, which were once filled by wrong choices, maybe wrong people, maybe things and situations which once served you, but moving forward they no longer do. Both grief and / or excitement can accompany an exploration of the questions of the first level.

> *"One door never closes without another opening."* — *Tasha's Grandmother.*
>
> *"If it doesn't open, it is not my door."* — *Unknown*
>
> *(Tasha's favourite present quote)*

Take a moment to respond to the questions. Note that there is a big difference between READING and DOING. Take the time to really DO the exercises suggested... just reading them is not enough. You want to take the time you need and get the full benefit of generating the answers for each question.

There will be different types of activities suggested throughout the system. You will have your favourite ones. You may need to close your eyes and see what it looks like. You may choose to write. You may want to sit back and think about it. You may want to read them out loud.

We recommend that you take these processes and exercises seriously and take the time to do them with care. Do them when you are relaxed and have time to do them with purpose. First you will decide what you want your focus to be for the exercises, and what you want to work on. Be specific and focus on fixing one problem at a time. Remember the wheel?

When you do the exercises, remember to be daring and ask for the most amazing outcome. Even if you don't know how to 'cook' it, place your order. If you can dream it, that means it is on the menu and your chef knows how to make it.

Remember the client Nathalie coached who wanted to find a boyfriend? She had pictured a perfect outcome and actually met a man that had everything on her list. All she had imagined was there. Only one problem: once she got it, she thought about something else she would have liked to be on the list. She called Nathalie asking what to do. First of all, as mentioned, there is no failure, only feedback. This was great news. It meant that it had worked. She had been able to find what she wanted. Nathalie told her to do the process again and add on to her outcome the things that she had left out. Her first reaction was: "Well, I feel badly, this guy is quite nice, maybe he will do for a while, I don't know if I want to meet someone else right now... what will happen if I make a new list and then meet the guy that has everything? Then, I will have to drop my present boyfriend and I would feel really badly." Isn't that funny how she was now in full awareness of her power and was afraid to dare and to want more for her life because she was in a satisfying situation?

We also mentioned earlier in this book that everything and everybody are stepping stones towards something else. We grow, we evolve and we change. The first boyfriend she found was great. He served a great role in her life. He gave her the self-confidence to realize she could have more. She deserved more. Without him, she may not have found out. He was a stepping stone towards what was coming next for her. She would not be serving him by staying with him because she, also, was more likely a stepping stone in his life. They stayed together for a while and she decided to make another list to see what could happen. She found another guy and they are now travelling the world together. As it turned out, she dared and it happened. She was not serving her present boyfriend by staying with him. She too was only a stepping stone in his life.

DESIRE VS WANT

The System's name is D.N.A. The letter D is for Desire. Could it have been the WNA system? Where the letter W would have been what you Want? What is the difference between a Desire and a Want? How much more effective are desires when it comes to setting up goals?

Let's pretend you hear a friend say: "I want to see that movie, it sounds good. I will see if I can get to it sometime this week." Then another friend cuts the conversation and says: "Oh yes I heard about this movie. I absolutely have to see it. It sounds amazing! I have cleared my Tuesday night and I am going to the 6:50pm show." Which of the two friends do you think is more likely to see the movie? Which one seems to have the strongest desire to see it?

You want to make your *wanting to be successful* into a compelling *desire*. Be on a mission to achieve your desire. When something is important to you, you make it happen. It is not like something on your to-do list, like having to brush your teeth in the morning. It is talking to you from the inside and you know you must do it. You are compelled and there is nothing that will get in your way. How amazing is that? Desires are happening at an unconscious level. Remember when we talked about your logical mind and your unconscious mind? Remember what drives you? What is your emotional motive? You use your logical for your day-to-day and you tend to rely on it a lot. However, real change happens at an unconscious level. When your unconscious mind is set on something, it works in the background and executes the command. Can you imagine how great it will be when your wanting to be successful becomes something so compelling that you naturally feel the need to fulfill it and will do everything that needs to be done? This will happen at an unconscious level, behind the scenes.

Remember to include as much as you want on your wish list. Although we made the analogy of the kitchen renovations, this is quite different in the way that for your dreams, you have an open budget. No restrictions. Give yourself lots of choices. Make it amazing!

> *"If you can dream it, you can do it."* — *Walt Disney*

Create more choices and more opportunities for yourself. As people get better strategies, they will use them. If you get a tool, you will use it. In any field, the top people in that field are those who have the most variety in their behaviour. They have choices of behaviour that their colleagues don't.

Any time you limit your behavioural choices you give others the competitive edge. If you are able to respond to any situation in a variety of ways, you are more likely to get your outcome.

Make sure you plan to be flexible and adaptive and that you program your brain to like many different types of work. Aim for the least restrictions as possible.

Nathalie gives this example: "I try to sleep eight to nine hours every night. I believe that I am at my best when I am well rested. However, if for some reason and unexpected circumstances I get only six hours of sleep, I also have a back-up belief that I am totally capable of functioning well and still be alert and capable of handling anything when I don't get as much sleep. I also believe that I will always be able to catch up on sleep and if I get fewer hours, each of the hours that I actually get will be very restful and recharging."

Eliciting a well-formed outcome on paper is a great way to start the programming process. You have more likely heard of SMART (specific, measurable, achievable, realistic, timely) Goals. This method is similar in some ways.

You have probably also heard of 'the list' that we do when we want something or 'vision boards'. These are great tools when they are correctly elicited and followed by the next steps necessary to bring them to life. These vision boards and smart goals differ from the DESIRE part of the system in the sense that our system is based on how your brain processes information. It follows the layers of your internal reality. Furthermore, the D.N.A. System offers you two more levels. This book takes life where most other literature ends. Deciding what you want is only the first step. We will also allow your DESIRE to sink in by showing you how to clean-up your old-self with the NEW YOU section, and then integrate the concepts in the ACTUALIZE section in order to bring your goal to life. A folder full of images and thoughts is just that. A folder. It needs to be implemented in order to really take life. But let's not jump ahead too much here. Let's start at the beginning and let's start filling up that folder.

Let's have a look at one more very important detail about the quality of material that you will be using to fill your folder.

CHAPTER 22

STAY AWAY FROM WHAT YOU DON'T WANT

"Success Tip: Don't focus on what you DON'T want. The reticular activation system is really good at what it does — if you unwillingly tell it to go search for trouble, heartache, or disappointment, it will absolutely find it, guaranteed, EVERY time." — John Assaraf

In order to express what they want, a lot of people use what they don't want. When you ask people what they want or what they desire, most people respond with a negative affirmation telling what they don't want. They want to stop being unsuccessful. They want to stop feeling ashamed. They want to not feel intimidated by new prospect clients. Nathalie's clients sit in her office and seek her help for what they don't want. They don't want to be stressed, they want to stop being impatient with their kids and they are tired of rushing everywhere all the time. Nathalie's go-to question is always: "What do you want instead?"

Defining our desire is really important. It is as if you were to ask your interior designer, who is helping you remodel your kitchen, that you want them to paint the kitchen 'not blue'. Can you imagine the margin of error that is possible here? Even if you say that you would like the kitchen to be green. There are so many different types of green that it is necessary to be specific when it comes to what you want.

You see a glass at the edge of the counter. You tell yourself that more likely it will fall on the floor and splash all over the whole kitchen. A moment later, you turn around and hit the glass 'by accident'. Or you see a report that you need to take to the office with you and you tell yourself: "I can't forget that tomorrow. If I do, I will be in big trouble at the office." The day after, you show up at the office and you forgot the report that you actually 'programmed yourself to forget'.

The words you use to make your demands to your brain matter. Whatever you focus on, you will get. What shows up in your mind if we tell you: "Do not make a mental picture in your head of Mickey Mouse dancing in a yellow Tuxedo." Did you see it? Of course you did. Even if we said: "Do NOT visualize it." You get what you concentrate on. The reason you saw it is because you had to process the information and then process the '*do not*' visualize it.

We have learned that our personal assistant is always listening. Our brain is making us right. If somewhere in your mind you have a belief that you're a loser and your brain hears it over and over, then your brain will make you right. If for the past 15 years you have been looking at yourself in the mirror. every day telling yourself: "I am clueless!" or "I am always going to be struggling" or "I am always behind and overwhelmed", you know, all these discriminating thoughts we say and tell ourselves? Well the brain hears it loudly and clearly, and it does everything it can to make you right!!! If you focus on not being a failure and not struggling, your brain hears *failure* and *struggle*.

First of all, with a mind set of being a failure, and your brain wanting to make you right, it will never really ask you to do anything that could make your career plum; it is doing everything it can to make you right and keep you struggling, because that is what you are conditioned to be. You are thinking about yourself as a person living from paycheque to paycheque and that is the way it is.

Let's say that you kick butt for a while and you actually take a course on marketing, attend seminars, hire a coach and you start being successful. Then your brain is panicking because it is saying: "oh no!... What is going on?... She is being successful and she is supposed to be a failure. What can I do...to make her right about struggling? Oh... here is a client coming, I'm gonna make her say something very embarrassing so that she humiliates herself and stops trying so hard." So we feel like we are sabotaging ourselves but the truth is that we are only making ourselves right about our thoughts.

Here is a great example that has probably already happened to you millions of times. You opened the fridge, looking for the water jug, and did not see it at first glance. You said out loud: "I can't find it" and you kept repeating it in your brain: "I can't see it, it is probably empty and in the sink or in the dishwasher. I can't find it." Then your spouse comes behind you and takes it right in front of your eyes. It was on the shelf, eye-level right in front of you but you had stopped your brain from seeing it. When you started saying 'I can't see it',you were making yourself right by not seeing it.

Your brain will always make you right. We have to be really careful with the thoughts and words we put into our brain. We have to be careful about what we want to be right.

> *"Whether you think you can or you can't, you're right either way."*
> *Henry Ford*

Be careful when you think. We tend to use the 'do-not' way too often. We try to stay away from what we don't want instead of thinking with positive words. Focus on the right things and with the proper mind set and your brain will make it easy. In the next chapter, we will ask you what you want. Make sure you remember to respond in the positive.

KEY CONCEPTS

When asked what they want, most people respond with what they don't want.

Using do-not in our language is not serving our cause even if our intentions are positive.

When programming ourselves with what we don't want, our brain is creating a model of reality that is not serving us and is making us right about it.

CHAPTER 23

AWARENESS - ENVIRONMENT
WHERE ARE YOU NOW?

"To be fully alive, fully human and completely awake is to be continually thrown out of the nest. To live fully is to be always in no-man's land, to experience each moment as completely new and fresh. To live is to be willing to die over and over again." — *Pema Chodron, From 'When Things Fall Apart'*

Let's start our work at the bottom of the pyramid, in the environment level of the brain. The first step is to bring awareness of your current situation and your surroundings.

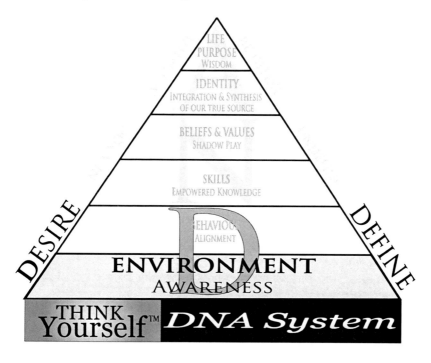

We will help you discover where you are 'now', and guide you towards where you want to see yourself. It is important to first DEFINE where you 'are', or how you presently see yourself and the people around you.

What do you want? Allow the first thing that pops into your head to be the answer.

> *Example: 'I want to know how to be successful' or 'I want to learn what success means to me'. 'I hate my job and I want to start loving it', 'I want to meet someone with whom to share my life and I feel that if I am successful, I will be more attractive to eventual prospects' 'I am intrigued by this Thinking Yourself Successful idea and I want to know what this is all about', or 'I am a wellness professional and I am always interested in reading new things that I could bring to my own clients'.*

When you know why, it's easier to stay focused and achieve success. It's important to know why you want to be successful. What is the first thing that comes to your mind? What is your outcome? What do you expect?

Why do you want to be successful?

> *Example: I want to be successful so I can and will....*
>
> *... have more fun at work*
>
> *... get up in the morning and feel driven and excited about my day*
>
> *... be organized and have time to enjoy my family and friends*
>
> *... feel that I am achieving something bigger than myself*
>
> *... feel that what I am doing counts and matters*
>
> *... live a long and stress-free life*

Okay, you have responded to the two big questions already. What and Why? Is that it? Are we done here? Guess what, we will ask you again and again. This is just a start. Your unconscious mind loves repetition. If you are faced with a question and you feel you have already responded, take a deep breath and ask your unconscious mind to give you another answer. The repetition is voluntary. Even if your logical mind thinks that you have already responded to this, keep going and go through all the questions.

At the base of the System, we start by answering questions about our environment and awareness. We need to get awareness of where we are and get the details of it on paper before we can incorporate that neurological level into our life. We will ask you questions about your environment and that will allow you to choose what influences you will allow into your life. Sometimes, what or whom we allow into our lives gives us clues as to how we feel about ourselves, both positively and negatively. This awareness is crucial and foundational to our success on every level.

Question: What in your environment needs an overhaul?

Example: I have a few people in my life who are very negative, or they do not respect my time. I need to either find a way to change the relationship dynamic, or start to weed them out of my life.

_____

_____

What are you aware about your current situation? Where are you at now regarding your goal?

Example: "I am just starting my career." "I have been successful before but seem to have lost my way."

_____

_____

How do you know you are not successful now?

Example: "I know because I feel stressed all the time and never have time to enjoy life."

_____

_____

Question: What in your environment supports your best Self?

Example: "I feel great about myself whenever I go to my favourite fitness class. I am surrounded by like-minded people and I feel strong, confident and capable when I leave, ready to tackle my day!"

_____

_____

How have you built or are you building strong structures and frameworks to support and sustain yourself?

Example: "I have started spending more time with a fantastic group of women entrepreneurs. We support and celebrate each other and do not compete. I have a new boyfriend, who loves my view on life. It is so much healthier for me than the last one who criticized everything I did."

_____

_____

What or who in your environment can help you identify what you need to work on?

Example: "I have a hard time getting along with a co-worker. My house is a mess all the time."

_____

_____

What events happened in your past that could have influenced where you are now? What changed in your life? Is there anything worth mentioning that could be linked to where you currently are?

> *Example: "I moved." "I got a new job." "I met someone." "I got married." "I got separated." "I had a child." "My kids moved away for school." "I had a tragedy in my life." "My father passed away."*

_____

_____

What is the relationship between these events and your current situation?

> *Example: "After I had my kids, I changed my priorities to serve the needs of my children and stopped focusing on my career"*

_____

_____

Think about the people in your environment, your parents, siblings, friends and partner. What is the relationship between these people (mother, father, brother, friend, etc.) and your current situation?

> *Example: "My father used to say that in order to be successful, you have to have connections and work from 5am until 10pm.... I don't have any connections and I don't want to work fifteen hours a day, so I will never be successful."*

_____

_____

Which of my relationships, work or personal, support my goals?

> *Example: "My husband is very supportive of my career and allows me time to work on it while he takes the kids to their sports and*

extra-curricular activities." "My parents are my biggest cheerleaders and always support me with everything I do."

How have I taught people how to treat me?

Example: "I always put my hand up to help others and do more than my share, therefore, people expect me to be the one that will take care of everything. Sometimes I wish someone else would take the lead."

Where do I need to draw a line in the sand and create more distance?

Example: "I have a very negative friend who tends to deflate me whenever I talk about my goals". "I spend so much time responding to other people's priorities that I tend to forget about my own."

Is there anything relevant about your childhood in relation to your present situation?

Example: "My mother was a career woman and was never home. We were raised by our nanny and always missed my mother." "Therefore, success comes with a high price. Success means, you never see your kids."

Who will be with you once you have achieved your goal?

Example: "I will be spending lots of time with my family". "I will be surrounded by positive and supportive people."

_____

_____

What will no longer be in your environment when you reach your goal?

Once you have reached your success goal, what will be missing that is currently present? What is in your life now that will not be there once you're successful?

Example: "I won't have to worry about paying my bills anymore". "I won't be exhausted all the time". "I won't let people dump their priorities over mine all the time"

_____

_____

What areas in my life make me feel strong and balanced?

Example: "When I am with my kids, I know I am a great mom and it makes me feel amazing. I wish I could feel that confident at work."

_____

_____

This begins the 'practice of awareness' and also clearly DEFINING who we are, who and what supports the best and most successful vision we have of ourselves.

Getting to know ourselves is awesome isn't it? We will continue to ask you several questions throughout the book. This was only level one.

KEY CONCEPTS:

AWARENESS

The first level at the bottom of the pyramid is the environment that helps us to become AWARE of the environments we create and participate in, and awareness about who we see ourselves to be in relation to all of it.

There are clues in our environment that guide us to understand what we want.

Questioning ourselves about our current situation helps us determine what we want.

Becoming Aware of what surrounds us and who is in our environment are the first steps in re-training the brain to allow transformation to happen.

Going over the elements and people in your life that have affected your present situation is helpful to understand what led you to where you are now.

This is the starting point and foundation for all future work in this book.

CHAPTER 24

ALIGNMENT - BEHAVIOURS
WHAT DO YOU DO?

"The essential element of successful strategy is that it derives its success from the differences between competitors with a consequent difference in their behaviour." — *Bruce Henderson*

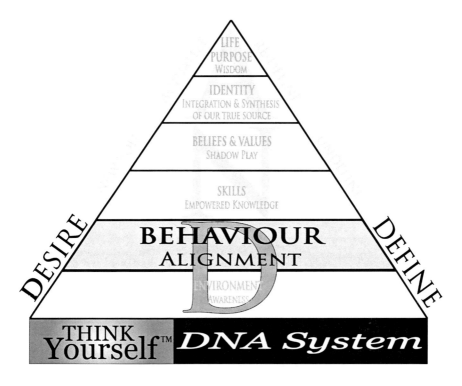

Now that we are aware of our environment and know where we are, we will get into the second neurological level: BEHAVIOURS. We will now aim for greater alignment in what we do. The behaviours, our daily actions, will be our best allies in our journey to success. We now start to lay down the tracks of a path where we choose and adopt new and successful behaviours.

The behaviour level includes our actions; what we do for a living, how we interact with those around us, plans, action along with successful or self- sabotaging behavioural choices.

This part is about the actions and choices we make. Our goal is to make them consistent and supportive of what we want in our lives. We seek to reflect on our behaviours to discover how well aligned they are with what we say we want.

Just like when we exercise or when we do yoga, we practice muscle definition and aim to bring our bodies into alignment. Following the same analogy, we can compare the behaviours we want to add to our success routine, but don't have yet, to muscles that are not being used and can atrophy in three weeks. Our unwanted behaviours are equivalent to poor postural habits and misalignments. Indeed, moves that are performed incorrectly, such as a bad running technique or lifting heavy weights without the proper form, create imbalance and a higher risk for injury. If we continue with our negative behaviours and keep giving in to bad habits, the imbalances in our life will keep taking over our chances of reaching our goals.

When our minds and habits are out of alignment with our dreams of success, it is like trying to hang a beautiful yoga posture on a posturally-compromised body. It doesn't fit well and certainly is not sustainable. Luckily we now know that the brain is malleable and we are not stuck with a brain that has been conditioned to sabotage our success. We can rebuild those muscles and recondition our minds to create something beautiful and sustainable for ourselves.

"I protect my right to recondition and re-invent myself. I have the strength and clarity to assess and re-asses when I am in alignment and moving from my true centre." — *Tasha Hughes*

What do I like to do?

Example: "I like to walk my dog" "I like to be involved in a group project at work" "I like to prepare a presentation".

_____

_____

What do I do that is fun?

Example: "I like to read fiction books" "I like going to the movies" "I love to travel".

_____

_____

Where do I need to bring my behaviours into greater alignment?

Example: "At work, I need to be better at focusing on the job at hand." "I need to take better care of my health."

_____

_____

Are my daily actions consistent with supporting that new alignment for success?

Example: "When I have a specific task to do, it seems to be taking me a lot of time to get started. I read emails instead, respond to posts and let other things get in the way of the important thing I have to do." "At home I am very strict about my diet, but when I go out, I seem to always order bad food."

_____

_____

We will now introduce a few questions which will require you to time-shift yourself in the future, having reached your goal. We will ask you about time frame, evidence and proofs of reaching that goal. For example, if your goal was to own a Mercedes Benz, some people would say that they will know they have reached their goal when they signed the contract of purchase for the car. Some other people would say they would have reached their goal when the salesman at the dealership gives them the keys to the car. Some people would say that they will know they have achieved their goal when they leave the parking lot, driving their new ride.

When and how do you want your outcome?

Decide on a realistic time frame to achieve your goal. What is your deadline? How will this happen?

> *Example: "I want the empowerment feeling of success to kick in right away." "I want to have my business plan defined by the end of next month". "It will happen step by step as I will be dedicating time to make it happen"*

_____

_____

What will you accept as evidence that you have achieved your outcome?

What evidence will you accept that lets you know when you have the outcome? Ensure that your evidence criteria are described in sensory-based terms i.e.: That which you can see, hear and/or touch that proves to you that you have done what you set out to do.

> *Example: "I will start smiling on my way to work." "I will be happy on a Monday morning". "I will see in my bank account the number I have been looking for." "I will receive recognition by my peers" "I will sign this important contract I have been wanting".*

_____

_____

How will you know that reading this book will have put you closer to your success? What needs to happen when you finish reading that will prove to you that you attained something valuable?

Example: "I will have a clear vision of what I want." "I will feel empowered" "I will be setting up some time to work on my goals" "I will be free of my limiting beliefs and will think differently about my own potential"

_____

_____

What do you want to change about your present behaviours?

Example: "I want to do what I know I should be doing" "I want everything I do to be in line with what I want"

_____

_____

What do you need to 'feed' or nourish yourself?

Example: "I need to sign up at a women's association and attend meetings on a regular basis to keep feeding myself with like-minded individuals"

_____

_____

In order for you to get want you want, the emphasis needs to be on you. Let's take for example the list that one of my clients made of her special desired soul mate. She had made the list of how she wanted him to be. How she wanted him to look, what she wanted him to do and how she wanted him to dress. The problem here is that the list can never be about what you want in others. It has to be about YOU. So instead of writing: "I want him to be tall, brown hair and have a great job", she re-wrote her list using herself instead of him. She wrote instead: "I find him very attractive, I am happy with him, he makes me feel secure as he has a great job, he tells me that he loves me, etc." We can program our own brain to how we want to feel, what we want to see and hear, but we cannot program somebody else's brain.

Remember, you have to be able to personally do, authorize or arrange it. Anything outside your control is not 'well formed'. Registering for a seminar is within your control. As is hiring a coach. Asking your employer for time off is not. The time off will only become well formed if it is granted. For example, it is hard to predict that your family will also be happy with your changes. It would be a mistake to state that on paper, the same as it would be a mistake to predict the weather. Your well-formed outcome is about you and you have to be able to control it.

Is it possible for a human being to achieve the outcome? If someone has done it, then in theory you can do it, as well. If you are the first, find out if it is possible. We do believe in the power of the brain and we believe that anything is possible, however, if your goal is to jump off a cliff and take off flying, you might want to re-write your goal. If your goal is to make two hundred million dollars in a month, you might want to reconsider putting something reasonably achievable in there. It must be something that is humanly possible, and that you could potentially do it. Your outcome has to be within the realm of human capability. If it is doable, then your brain can make you dream it and can make you right.

Is it achievable?

Example: "Yes, in fact, my neighbour has done it!" "Yes, of course it is because my goal is to feel self-confident and at a point in my life I was. So I know it is possible for me to get it back."

_____

_____

We now invite you to a mental exercise. As mentioned earlier, your unconscious mind can process over two million pieces of information every second. When you use your logic and write one answer, you more likely lose over a million of details, images, sounds, feelings that also came to mind as you were responding to the question. Remember that your brain can process information so much faster that you can write or express it on paper. Now take a moment to close your eyes and use your senses to add details. What will you see, hear and feel when you have your goal?

Make a mental image of your outcome. Add on all the details you need to make it more compelling. This question will be done in your head. See your outcome happening. See it as if it is happening now. Add on more details based on your senses. What else do you see? What do you hear? What are you saying in your head? How do you feel? Place that image on a giant screen and turn up the dial. Add on everything you need to make it nicer, brighter, more compelling, dare to dream everything you want to be part of this picture. See yourself as a third person looking at you in the picture. Once you have seen everything you needed to see, heard everything you needed to hear and felt everything you needed to feel, take the picture and insert it in your timeline in your future. It is like placing the picture as a to-do list for your personal assistant. You are telling your unconscious mind that this is what will happen in your future. Your unconscious mind will keep working on achieving the result as it was just told that this was going to happen. Your brain doesn't know the difference between reality and fiction. It just executes what you tell it that is going to happen.

"Nothing happens unless first a dream."   — *Carl Sandburg*

Once you have opened the pipeline of ideas, you are ready for the next chapter where you will write your positive outcome.

KEY CONCEPTS:

Aligning our behaviours with our goals lays down the foundation for great serving habits.

Giving yourself deadlines and guidelines about what to look for when your goal will be achieved contributes to making your goals concrete and realistic.

Mentally rehearsing what you want, making your goal compelling using all senses will start making it real in your head.

CHAPTER 25

YOUR POSITIVE OUTCOME

"The universe buries strange jewels deep within us all, and then stands back to see if we can find them." — Elizabeth Gilbert

It is now time to write the software that will reprogram your brain to make the jump into a more successful fishbowl. You can use a recap of everything you discovered in the previous exercises to write down the perfect success in the context you are considering. State what you want in positive terms. i.e. What do you want? Where do you want it? When do you want it? Example: "I want to be, do or have X". If the answer forms as "I do not want..." then ask yourself: "What do I want instead of..." If it feels totally untrue when you say it out loud, you may want to start your statement with: "I am willing to learn how it feels to be successful." Giving you permission to evolve.

Examples:

"My name is... and I am feeling great in my office. It is time to meet a very important potential client and I know I am fully prepared and ready. I will wow them and leave the meeting with a signed contract! I got this. I am confident and I can't wait to tell my family tonight at dinner as I am loving my new schedule of taking the time to enjoy the evening meal every day with them."

Example of someone whose daughter's wedding is coming up: "My name is ……….. and I am looking great and feeling great in my mother of the bride's dress that I am wearing at my daughter's wedding in July. I am at peace as everything is ready and perfectly planned. I have time to enjoy myself and take full advantage of this perfect day where love is embracing everybody. People are telling me how fabulous I look. I feel proud and happy to have had the time to be involved in the planning as my successful career allowed me to take the time. I can see my daughter being at her best and tremendously happy. I can smell the scents of the flowers on this gorgeous July day and I have a wonderful feeling going through my body that will keep me happy for years to come."

"My name is.... and I am in control of my days. I love that I live only a few minutes away from my work and I am really focused and can get a lot done in a single day. Every day when I leave my office, I feel that I have achieved much, and that my work made a difference for someone else. I have time to exercise and eat well and I am in the best shape of my life. I have achieved a work-life balance and my relationship with my significant other is very fulfilling. I always have time and the money to attend unexpected events or expenses for myself or my family and I always discover what to do and how to be flexible and adapt. I am truly, genuinely happy. I hear people tell me how great I look and I feel amazing. I love myself."

"My name is.... and I love my new life. I have successfully changed my old behaviours into new habits that are serving me. I can breeze through life in a light way and I have the self-confidence to introduce myself to highly intelligent, attractive and motivated people like me. I am happy to be surrounded by positive influences that keep me on track with my new choices. I always find ways to stay motivated and inspired."

Your turn, write your positive outcome:

My name is _____ and I ... _____

_____

_____

_____

_____

_____

_____

_____

_____

Once you have written your outcome, place copies of this statement all over your house, in every room and in your car. Write everything as if it's happening in the present, as if it's happening right now.

You can add to your statement as time goes by. It is always good to keep it updated and make sure that your statement changes and evolves with you and your changing desires.

Read this statement several times a day and at least once out loud so that your brain hears it out loud. There is a popular belief that it takes 21 days to re-create new neural pathways through the brain, to create the new habit. This statement came from Doctor Maxwell Maltz in the 1950s from a research with patients that were receiving plastic surgery.

It would take them, on average, 21 days to get their new nose for example.[4]

As you can realize now, this research, although quite popular, is quite dated. I prefer to follow the results of Doctor Phillippa Lally who conducted a research in 2009 with volunteers who chose an eating, drinking or activity behaviour to carry out daily, in the same context for 12 weeks. The study published in the European Journal of Social Psychology reported that the average time to reach automaticity for performing an initially new behaviour was 66 days.[5]

So read it for at least 2 months (66 days). If you catch yourself thinking negative thoughts, turn them into positive thoughts. It took years for you to get where you are now, it might take a few months to reset your brain and create new habits.

We are about to start cleaning your brain to make room for your new outcome in the NEW YOU section of the D.N.A. System. We will also anchor your positive outcome in the ACTUALIZE section. What you have done so far was to tell your brain what you DESIRE.

As you go through the next steps of the System, continue to read your outcome many times per day. This will help your brain to be well wired and well programmed to always continue working on it, whether you are conscious about it or not. You know how sometimes you think about a song and you just cannot get the title of the song, you can't seem to remember it? Then you stop thinking about it and it comes back two hours later? Well, in fact, although you think that you stopped thinking about it, your brain (your personal assistant) kept working on it, it never stopped looking for the title as you had ordered it to do so when you said: "I will remember it later." So a brain that is well wired will always deliver and follow the ultimate order without being distracted by irrelevant or unimportant things.

---

[4] http://jamesclear.com/new-habit
[5] https://www.ucl.ac.uk/news/news-articles/0908/09080401

Here is a concrete example of how a brain that is programmed for something will follow the ultimate goal as opposed to being distracted by a short-term gain. Nathalie, who thinks that she is the luckiest person in the world and that she always gets what she wants, tells the story: "A few years ago we were in Mexico with a group. Our friends were all going to a restaurant at night. They had reserved for the 10 of them and we wanted to join them so we tried to get the reservation changed to 12 and even though I used my Spanish to negotiate with the waiter, nothing worked! They said they simply could not accommodate 12 of us. So my husband and I had to eat somewhere else that night. Let me tell you that I was ticked off... It was impossible. How could this be happening? I always get what I want! Well, the day after, at the hotel, everybody was sick with food poisoning."

THE RETICULAR ACTIVATING SYSTEM.

We have a very small part of our brain called the Reticular Activating System (RAS). The RAS pays attention both to our environment, as well as to where we tend to place our attention (needs, wants, desires). It is always assessing and discerning what is relevant and important, in order to keep us safe AND help to get us what we want.

In the example above, Nathalie, who has programmed her brain to be safe and healthy, somehow must have picked up on things that she was not even aware. Maybe she glanced through the kitchen and her unconscious mind noticed that the meat was stored on the counter and not in the fridge. Maybe one of the two millions things she overheard with her unconscious mind, as she was walking to the restaurant, was someone saying they had been sick eating there before, or it could have been anything. Nathalie's RAS protected her from being sick.

There you have it! If you are well programmed, you don't need to think about it anymore. Your brain works for you and makes things happen for you. Even if you don't see it right away.

Some people call it the Universe, some people call it God. Everybody has a different name for when these things happen. We just like to think that these instances are just another example of how powerful our brain is.

KEY CONCEPTS

YOUR POSITIVE OUTCOME

Use every thought you have generated so far to write down a positive outcome that will satisfy your desires.

Once you have elicited your outcome, continue to read it and keep letting your brain know that this is what you want.

Knowing what you want and writing your expectations & desires will set the tone for the unconscious mind to open the gate to new possibilities.

PART 6:
THE "N"

CHAPTER 26

NEW YOU - UNDEFINE

"Do not fear to lose what needs to be lost." — *Unknown*

Now that you have completed the D part of the D.N.A. System, you know who you are and what you want. In the NEW YOU section, you'll be introduced to a cleanup phase, necessary before installing your desires.

We will study the next two layers of your brain. The Skills level will give you Empowered Knowledge and the Beliefs and Values level will allow you to unravel deeper layers of yourself through the Shadow Play exercises.

You will find out how you create your own model of reality. Sometimes we imagine constraints and barriers that do not exist. They may just be in our heads. You will discover how to turn the negative into positive, how to change your nemesis into a NEW YOU by neutralizing the past.

The second step of the D.N.A. System is to make room to implement what you just elicited. Your unconscious mind has already started to work on your desires. Your outcome has been planted and now we need to make sure that there is plenty of space for your outcome to grow. Just like in our original example, in order to get the new dream kitchen, you need to do some demolition and get rid of the out-dated cupboards. When you are planning a kitchen renovation, you will more likely make some sort of folder where you will file samples of the cupboards to match the backsplash, the tile, the paint colours, the type of granite for the countertop, hardware samples, etc. This is what you have just done. You have just made your folder and filled it with what you want. The reality is: it is just a folder. It is not a new kitchen. You cannot cook and entertain people in that folder. There is still a lot of work to be done in

order to get to your real life-size kitchen. When a lot of books end after the folder has been made, THINK Yourself™ SUCCESSFUL continues and guides you to the next steps to concretize your dream.

Rest assured that all of the methods and processes that we use are light and effortless. When working with a new client, Nathalie sometime can sense their stress level rising when she mentions this part. They think that she will psychoanalyze their past and they will have to re-live their negative experiences and dig through the dirt, and cry and suffer until the demons have been exorcised. Please. Relax. You are not about to do any of this. This is the best part. The clearing section is empowering, insightful, cleansing and most of all, fun and easy!

KEY CONCEPTS

NEW YOU

You have elicited your desire and now is time to make some room in order for your outcome to have space to be implemented

CHAPTER 27

SKILLS - EMPOWERED KNOWLEDGE

"It is possible to fly without motors, but not without knowledge and skill." — *Wilbur Wright*

The third neurological level, skills and capabilities, leads to empowered knowledge.

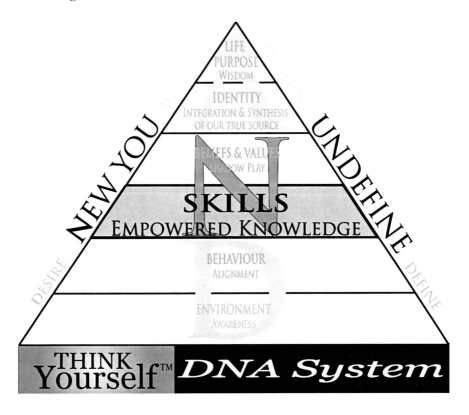

From a neuroscience perspective, we are starting to soften and disengage the old neural pathways. It is imperative at this point that we REWIRE. And so begins the very exciting process of REINVENTION!

We invite you now to start to embrace your own unique strength and simultaneously unravel and disengage from impairments to your growth and progress. This can be both exhilarating and scary! Be assured, it will pay off! Stay the course to your own greatest success.

Living in mastery at the level Empowered Knowledge means allowing the greatest vision you have of yourself to support your intentions of living your life in your own integrity. The Empowered Knowledge questions will guide you through discovering your skills and refining them.

Write down what you do very well, the skills you do effortlessly. Think of the things people say about you when they are astonished with your talent or your finished product: "I don't know how you do it! There is no way I could do this." That means it is a skill. Everybody can brush their teeth, which is a behaviour, but not everybody can remember the words of all the songs they hear. That is a skill.

What skills come easily and are effortless for you? Name some things you do well:

Example: "I organize my days" "I can see the big picture when it comes to a project" "I like working methodically"

_____

_____

How do you feel strong? Alive? In charge?

Example: "I feel great when I plan a party, because I am very good at it"

_____

_____

How are you now free to pursue greater skills and knowledge to move yourself into a bigger version of yourself?

Example: "I feel very confident and resourceful with the knowledge and skills I have accumulated over the last six months. I needed foundational tech knowledge, and now I feel I can shift from practical knowledge to idea implementation and content for my online courses."

Where do you trust yourself more and how are you making empowered choices?

Example: "I now allow myself to 'feel out' a situation. Even if I cannot put my finger on it, if a situation or relationship doesn't feel like a good choice for me, I will honour that voice and take it into consideration. In the past, I responded based on obligation or logic, even if I felt wrong (and it often ended poorly). The more I have done this, the faster and more clear those readings of my true feelings and desires become."

Do you have or can you obtain all the resources, both tangible and intangible that you need to achieve your outcome? Resources include knowledge, beliefs, objects, premises, people, money and time. Do you need to read some books on your specific domain? Do you need to subscribe to some podcasts or mindset websites or blogs that will feed you with information during your success journey? Do you need to hire a life coach that will create a specific program for you and help you stay on track?

Do you have all the resources you need to achieve your outcome?

Example: "Yes I do, I have been reading so many books, registered to so many seminars, now I realize that it is all inside of me." "I will hire a coach who will walk with me through the path towards my new life."

When do you use your gut feeling to make empowered choices? When do you know that you can fully trust yourself?

Example: "I am very confident in my ability to choose the people with whom I am friends or with whom I associate. My gut always tells me immediately if this is a good connection for me."

What do you want or need to learn now?

Example: "I need to learn how to give a better presentation." "I need to know how to connect my social media together." "I need to upgrade my PowerPoint skills"

Where are you edging towards taking greater risks?

Example: "I need to get out of my comfort zone when it comes to prospecting new clients".

In which ways do you now trust yourself that you did not before?

Example: "In looking at my 'have-done' list, I realize how much I have grown in the past year." "I would always ask a friend to come clothes shopping with me and now I trust myself to buy things on my own."

"I am strong. I trust IN MYSELF. I HAVE MY OWN BACK"
— *Tasha Hughes*

Now that you have defined what you want in the DESIRE section and equipped yourself with empowered knowledge in this section, you are able to cross the bridge between what you want and how to make the changes in your head in order for your unconscious mind to move in the same direction as your goals.

Here is a quick technique that you can use when facing a situation, to become more confident about your skills.

THE POWER OF THE PAUSE.

The Pause is a powerful tool to use, to stop, and become aware of our own thoughts and behaviours. In yoga, there is a reverence for the pause between the inhalation and the exhalation. The yogis say that it is in the pause where you will meet your Self; both your greatest fears and your highest potential.

From a neuroscience perspective, The Pause creates an opportunity to disengage from the old neural pathways, and begin to REWIRE and REINVENT. 'Neurons that fire together wire together' is a common saying in the field of brain science. The more we think or do anything, the stronger those pathways become. So the next time you find yourself saying or doing something that is inconsistent with where you want to go, intentionally create a Pause through the 'STIR" technique.

STIR stands for Stop, Interrupt, Replace

> *Example: I have to do a presentation at work for a prospective client. I love the concept I am presenting but I am terrible at public-speaking. I feel like a phony doing a 'pitch'.*
>
> *1) Stop and take a few deep breaths. Redirecting your focus to your breath instead of your thoughts will automatically help you to shift to a different part of your brain.*
>
> *2) Interrupt. Recognize that you want to cancel, change or re-wire that thought, and consider how to do that. You have now shifted from problem-seeking mode into problem-solving mode. Ask yourself how you might 'flip' this language and idea.*
>
> *3) Replace. "I love the concept. I will focus on having a conversation with this client to enthusiastically explain why I love it." Therefore, I will shift the focus away from feeling self-conscious, to the topic to be covered.*

With the empowered knowledge you gained from responding to the questions and learning about the technique to which you were just introduced, you now feel more powerful after the culmination of work from the first three levels. You are starting to get out of your old way and embrace the best parts of yourself.

KEY CONCEPTS

EMPOWERED KNOWLEDGE

Empowered Knowledge is truly about acknowledging your gifts and strengths, and from THAT place, trusting yourself to make more empowered choices from this moment forward.

CHAPTER 28

YOUR OWN MODEL OF REALITY

"You never really understand a person until you consider things from his point of view." — *Harper Lee*

EACH PERSON HAS HIS OR HER OWN UNIQUE MODEL OF REALITY

You have your own way of establishing your norm. Your world is quite different from everybody else. Empowered knowledge about your own model of reality is crucial in order to identify what needs to be undefined about your perspective about reality. Even if the Internet and its tools allow us now to see maps in real time, with landscapes and buildings, it is never like being there for real and if we are there for real, we never really get the full extent and all of the details of the location where we are. Even if you can make a mental picture of an apple, there is no apple in your head, it is not a real apple, it is only a picture of an apple.

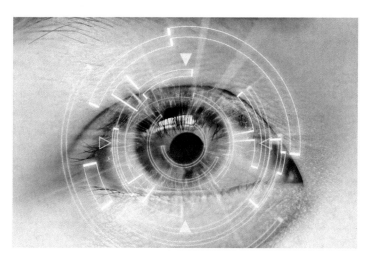

There is so much information thrown at us every second that we filter it and remember only a portion and make an idea for ourselves of what this place looks like. The map is not the territory. The way we represent the world refers to reality. It isn't reality itself. We don't respond to reality. We respond to our internalized map of reality. Interpretations may or may not be accurate. Our understanding of the world is based on our own experience and how we represent it. Whatever we think is going on, is just what WE think of it, it is not the real thing. That is our interpretation of how we see things.

Here is an easy way to represent this concept. Pretend that someone who is afraid of snakes sees a snake on the garden path. Their heart starts to beat faster, they start to sweat, the adrenaline goes up, the fear grows and their inner-self goes mad. Now, just as they are about to run as fast as they can in the opposite direction, they realize that it's a garden hose and suddenly feel completely better. In their model of reality, because they are afraid of snakes, their reality created a series of behaviours and they acted as if it was true. Your unconscious mind doesn't know reality. It only knows what you make of it.

We are all different. Some of us think in visual images. Some like sounds and words. Some are primarily aware of body sensations. When we map our world, we delete and restore information we receive through our senses. Then, when something happens to us, we quickly classify the experience based upon our pre-conceived idea on the subject. We distort everything to make it fit our reality. We tell ourselves a modified story of what happened. A story from which we have deleted, restored and generalized information.

> *Preconceived notions are the locks on the door to wisdom.*
> *— Mary Browne*

Let's say for example you have a belief that the whole world is against you. Whenever you see people that are there to help, you will delete them quickly and not pay attention to their offers to help you. You will distort people's comments to make them sound like they are out to get you, and you will generalize the one time that it happened, pretending that this is ALWAYS like this and make your belief true. We all have beliefs. The more we challenge them, the more we can see changes and transform our beliefs into more useful and resourceful ones. Our brain distorts reality and creates a new one, which results from that on which we focus.

Here is how the same event can create three different realities: Three friends go to a movie together. They all came out of the movie and really enjoyed it. When they respectively got home, they told the story of the movie to their significant other. The first woman told her husband how this overweight lady performed a great life lesson in this movie where being unattractive and overweight didn't keep her from succeeding in life.

The second lady tells her husband how this movie was about a very funny lady, that appeared to not be really serious about work, got herself into the corporate world with a good paying position even though she wasn't working 24/7 and still had time for her children.

The third lady told her husband that the story was about a woman who defied the male-dominated corporate world and got to the top of her firm, ahead of the men that were applying for the promotions.

If we tell you that one of the friends is overweight, one of them is a family-oriented woman and the one is a women's rights advocate, do you know which one is which? Do you see how you get to that which you focus? They all saw the same movie and somehow drew three different conclusions depending upon their own model of reality. Each of them is right as they are operating within their own reality.

Let's say you think you are a failure. When someone gives you a compliment and tells you: "Wow, you did amazingly today in the meeting", you complete the sentence in your head with "Yeah, she probably thinks that I am usually very stupid and she is trying to make me feel better." You have ignored the compliment, you have distorted it to fit your 'failure-reality' and you are now generalizing it and everything you hear is always about your failure.

In a seminar recently, Nathalie pointed at one of her participant's shirt - she was wearing a championship's slow-pitch jersey - and Nathalie was about to ask: "Are you still playing slow-pitch?" when the participant interrupted her sentence. Nathalie had time only to say: "Are you still....." and the participant said: "Pregnant? No I am just fat." Interesting how her own model of reality made her think that Nathalie would even say something like that while she was just asking her if she still played baseball!

Now what if it did happen to you for real that someone once told you that you were a failure. That memory might be quite distorted. Maybe they said it just like that, or maybe they said, you are not at your best in this job description and you took it like an abrupt *you're a failure* comment. You only get affected if you believe that fits you. Change your belief and it won't affect you anymore. Instead, that kind of comment reinforces the belief and limits you. Then it is not long before all you can hear are comments about your failure even when they have nothing to do with it.

When we look at the same things with different perspective, the more detailed our map is, the more freedom and flexibility we get. We also have to make sure our map is up to date and do a reality check from time to time. Have you ever been caught by a GPS when it takes you somewhere not knowing about the new road that has been built? Then it goes "*recalculating*" on you?

Sometimes we imagine constraints and barriers that do not exist. We try something that did not work before and keep doing the same thing. If nothing changes, nothing changes. There is a popular definition of insanity and it's to do the same thing over and over and expect different results. What that really means is that we keep trying to change our behaviours when what we need to change is our beliefs. Our future has not been read yet. Let's not let anyone, not even our own map, convince us on the contrary. It is not about who is right and who is wrong and it is not about what is true either. A map helps us feel resourceful and makes us see things from a different perspective. What people say they do and think they do is often far from what they actually do.

"Beliefs have the power to create and the power to destroy. Human beings have the awesome ability to take any experience of their lives and create a meaning that disempowers them or one that can literally save their lives." — *Tony Robbins*

If we are operating within our model of reality, then we are always right. Our mental map limits what we're capable of, more often than external reality limits us. If we have obstacles in our head, they are worse than the external reality. There's always going to be an excuse, and it's our brain and mental map that creates the excuse.

In your model of reality, whatever works for you will show up. Let's say you have never noticed the brands of cars that were driving by you every day on your way to work. All of a sudden, as you are shopping for a BMW X1, they start popping out everywhere. You start seeing them all the time, everywhere! Do you always happen to notice your own car - or similar - when you drive by your 'twin'?

Once well programmed, trust your own model of reality to tell you what to do with everything that you see and that is stored inside you. We will teach you how to put your model of reality to service and change that model of reality to better suit your desires. If you live in a model that says that you are successful and healthy, you will suddenly start noticing the opportunities to thrive (instead of finding excuses). You will be spending more time building great long lasting habits and not even think about wasting time on social media, other than for when you choose to spend time on it. Allow your unconscious mind to do the necessary tweaking that will serve you even better. In order to do that, we need to work with the neurological levels of the mind.

KEY CONCEPTS

YOUR OWN MODEL OF REALITY

We all have our own model of reality and when we operate within our own model, we are always right.

Working on changing our model of a reality that doesn't serve us, using the neurological levels, will contribute to creating a new reality where success can grow and become a part.

CHAPTER 29

BELIEFS & VALUES
SHADOW PLAY

"No one can make you feel inferior without your consent"
— *Eleanor Roosevelt*

Let's do a bit of cleaning. Even if you have some new cupboards to replace the old ones, it doesn't mean that there is room in your kitchen to keep them all - old and new ones. We need to remove the unwanted limiting beliefs and create more space for the new beliefs to take roots.

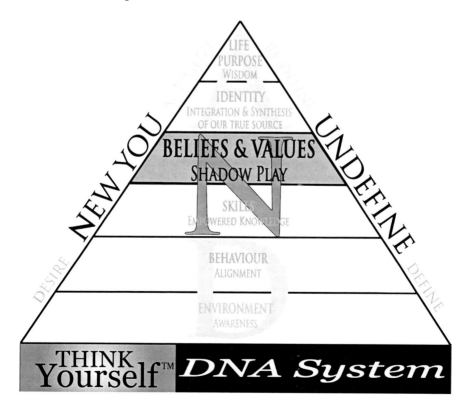

The following questions will teach you how to identify what is important to you. What you believe to be true, what you value, what you would defend, what you used to perceive as your limitations, your weaknesses, your boundaries and mostly your potential.

You will discover that you can be whatever you want to be. This section will help you shake the box so that you can get out of it. It is like taking a crow bar and lifting the old counter top so that it is easier to remove. It will soften your limits and help you see yourself from your core, from within as opposed to see yourself from the outside, looking at your limitations.

Shadow Play is really an invitation to 'sit with' those deeper fears of the unconscious, to breathe through the fear, and to come out the other side, galvanized.

Now that you have successfully been through the first three layers of the System, you will agree that the questions in this section allow you to dig further and answer them from a deeper place.

What do you consider sacred?

Example: "My freedom. I always need to be able to make my own schedule."

_____

_____

What do you value most?

Example: "My family" "A sense of achievement" "Having fun in everything I do"

_____

_____

What will you defend?

Example: "My children" "My integrity" "My opinion when I know I am right and it is 'the right' thing to do"

_____

_____

What do you 'stand' for?

Example: "Women's equality" "Helping the less fortunate"

_____

_____

What are your highest principles?

Example: "I will always find my way to peace." "I keep adapting and changing until I feel happy with what I am doing"

Where in your life are you no longer a victim?

Example: "I use to think that the guy I was with was taking advantage of me, until I realized I was the one giving him my power"

What have you been afraid to look at?

Example: "I know I am afraid to make a leap and quit my full time job to live from my personal business. I used to be afraid to even start looking at the possibility of it happening. I now feel that I should start the process and set goals for myself and set up what will need to happen for me to be able to live from my dream."

What do you want to let go of that you feel is holding you back?

Example: "I believe my fear of approaching new clients and selling my services is not serving my business"

What will come into your life that's currently missing?

Example: "I will have more self-confidence" "I will meet a boyfriend when I am successful" "I will be able to afford better holidays" "I will have time to run with my dog" "I will have time to focus on my health and finally lose the weight I gained when I had kids ."

How do you not feel worthy?

a) Where and when do you doubt yourself?

Example: "When I price my services, I feel that I am often under-evaluating myself"

---

b) Whose voice is STILL in your head telling you that you are not good enough?

Example: "I still hear one of my teachers telling me how I was totally off track" "I can hear my dad saying how important it is to get married and take care of my husband instead of doing something that I want to be doing."

---

c) What makes you want to run and hide?

Example: "I get intimidated when presenting to successful people. It is much easier to present to average-Joe type of crowd"

"The way of the warrior is to turn and face MYSELF. I turn and face my fears, knowing that I AM ENOUGH."   — *Tasha Hughes*

Where in your life do you find yourself doing the opposite of what you want to be doing, or know you should be doing, to support your future success?

Example: Often after lunch, I have to run an errand or do a delivery. En route, I go through the coffee shop drive-thru and grab a Caramel Explosion coffee with whipped cream and a S'mores cookie to go with it. This leaves me feeling (a) temporarily comforted ... which is quickly followed by (b) disgust at my lack of self-control. I KNOW it is the wrong choice. Emotionally, it leaves me feeling out of control, it ruins the healthy dinner I had planned for later, and I have noticed my skin is breaking out and my pants are becoming a bit snug.

What small, nagging voices remain, that can be in the way of reaching your outcome?

Example: "Even if everything tells me that I should go for it, there is still part of me that feels it is too risky and I won't be able to handle it."

What does achieving your goal do for you? Remember the secondary benefits: The intention behind the behaviour. What will achieving the positive outcome you wrote in chapter twenty-five do for you? What else will that bring you?

Example: "When I get this new contract, it will prove to me that I am able to land that kind of contract and empower me to prospect for more."

_____

_____

The next few questions are specific questions that will open your unconscious mind to dig deeper. They are being asked in opposite affirmations or negations to force your unconscious mind to dig for different answers. They are the Cartesian coordinates of the brain. Have fun with them and pay attention to the nuances in the questions. Remember that your unconscious mind loves that stuff. This could be the section that makes you generate the light bulbs you need to drive yourself to your outcome.

What will you gain if you have it?

Example: I will gain self-confidence

_____

_____

What will you lose if you have it?

Example: I will lose the heavy feeling that I carry around "The voice in my head telling me I am a failure will be gone" "The shame and feeling of being a fraud will be gone"

"The feeling of being forced into a job I hate will be gone" "I will not get to complain and have pity-parties anymore"

_____

_____

What will happen if you get it?

Example: "I will be happy with myself"

_____

_____

What won't happen if you get it?

Example: "I won't be ashamed of myself anymore"

_____

_____

What will happen if you don't get it?

Example: "I will continue feeling depressed and unhappy"

_____

_____

What won't happen if you don't get it?

Example: "I will never know if I had the capabilities, if I had it in me to reach it and will regret not trying." "I won't serve my life purpose of motivating and inspiring others."

_____

_____

The next questions are very important. Are all costs and consequences of achieving your outcome, including the time involved, acceptable to you and anyone else affected by it? This is known as ecology. Consider the costs, consequences, environmental and third party impact of having the outcome. Let's say you have wanted to separate from your spouse, as you believed your relationship was going down the drain. If you could be divorced right now, would you take it? Let's say the year of separation was over, the paperwork was done, the house was sold, you had moved into a new place and all was final. Would you be happy now? Or would you miss him terribly? Would you take it if it were handed on a silver platter to you right now?

If you could have it now, would you take it?

"Yes this is what I want and I am totally sure of it" "Mmm, I am not sure if that is what I really want".

The next question is to ensure that your outcome is worth the time, outlay and effort involved in achieving it, and that impact on third parties or the environment is accounted for. Your dream has always been to open your own aesthetics school but if you did so, you would never see your children, as you would be working every weekend. How about you plan for it and wait a few years once your kids are off to school before doing it? Would that be worth it then? Listen to what your values are telling you.

Are the costs and consequences of obtaining this outcome acceptable?

Example: "In order to invest in that new business, I would have to spend the money that I had initially saved for my children's education. Not worth it." "I had never thought about it this way but I may be holding a limiting belief about my only child to not receive the attention he needs if we have another baby. I need to accept this consequence in order to be able to get pregnant. He will then discover the valuable lesson of having a sibling. Totally worth it."

The next six questions are an overview of all the beliefs and values questions we have asked so far. In light of your previous answers, you will be amazed at how quickly you will find answers to this last series of questions.

CORE question: What do you believe you are and will always be?
Something you are, at your core, you are happy to be that way, as you want
to be like that, and you know in your core that you will always be it. What are
you proud and content to be?

Example: "Honest"

_____

_____

**POTENTIAL question: What is something you want to be and
believe you could become?** Something you are hoping to become.
Something you are excited about becoming.

Example: "Organized"

_____

_____

**LIMITATION question: What is something you want to be but
believe you are not?**
Something you see as your limit? You would like to be that way but you feel
trapped and frustrated as you don't seem to be able to be it.

Example: "Good with money"

_____

_____

**BOUNDARY question: What is something you don't want to be
and never will be?**
You don't want to be that way and you feel very strongly about never
becoming that way either. What is off limits? What is your boundary?
You don't ever want to be that way.

*Example: "I don't want to be working from five AM until midnight
every day."*

_____

_____

"You can waste your life drawing lines. Or you can live your life crossing them."   — Shonda Rhimes

WEAKNESS question: What is something you don't want to be but believe you could become? What is your weakness or your defect? Are you afraid you might become this? This may cause you anxiety as you don't want to be that way and you may become it.

Example: "I am afraid I could become sick from being so stressed out"

_____

_____

SHADOW question: What is something you don't want to be but you are afraid you are?

Something you feel guilty about, or of that which you are ashamed.

Example: "I am afraid I am lazy".

_____

_____

In light of all the questions you have responded to in this chapter, take a moment to reflect on what really resonates as something from this exercise that you will be interested in exploring later. Ask yourself what was your 'aha' moment? What is the golden nugget of this chapter? Remember which beliefs and values will be the saviour of your shadow.

More than likely, you now have a very different view of yourself. You have opened up the mental process and set up a path favourable to transformation. You have just pulled the old cupboards from the wall with a crow bar and now it will be much easier to remove them and get rid of them. Negative limits, shadows, weaknesses, defects or boundaries have been loosened up and they are ready to leave your body. This is what we will do in the next chapter.

KEY CONCEPTS

BELIEFS & VALUES - SHADOW PLAY

Understanding what we believe and what is important to us is the fuel that will continue to drive us towards success.

After the initial clarity, gains and strength achieved in the first three levels, deeper fears and demons will appear out of the shadows in an attempt to sabotage your success.

Facing the Shadow Play questions bravely will put you back in control, rather than your subconscious mind.

Using our core and our potential is the key to shift our limitations and boundaries. Once identified, we know in which area of our life we may hold negative limiting beliefs. When we choose to pay attention to these limiting beliefs, we can let go of our weaknesses and shadows and transform ourselves to what we really want to be.

CHAPTER 30

NEGATIVE EMOTION RELEASE TECHNIQUE

"Owning our story can be hard but not nearly as difficult as spending our lives running from it." — *Brene Brown*

This chapter is offering you a very powerful technique that will help you release everything you are now ready to let go of, and build a New You.

As mentioned in the Neural Pathways section, you have been going through life and have had different experiences that made you create limiting beliefs about yourself. From these beliefs, you generated some unwanted behaviours that turned into bad habits. Here is the good news. All these experiences were far from negative. They were only feedback.

They were only designed to make you learn something. When these experiences happened in your life, they were only there to get you to where you are today.

They happened to make you stronger and to make you grow. For every negative challenge that you experienced, a positive learning came with it. Unfortunately, this positive learning was attached to a negative feeling.

This exercise will help you detach the negative feeling from the positive learning so that you can let go of the negative feeling. We can make this negative feeling go away by telling the unconscious mind to acknowledge the positive learning from the challenge. Once this positive learning has been received, there is no need to keep the negative emotions anymore and your unconscious mind can release it.

> *"In the middle of every difficulty lies opportunity."*   — *Albert Einstein*

We recommend that you read the exercise a few times so that you know exactly what to do once you close your eyes. Remember that your unconscious mind can process 2.3 million pieces of information every second. Your unconscious mind will know exactly what to do. Your logical mind might try to get in the way. Just ignore it. Trust that your powerful unconscious mind knows what to do. Take a moment to relax and get into a calm state so that you can give your unconscious mind a favourable environment to do its magic. Uncross your legs, ground your feet and place your hands ever so lightly on your thighs. Take a few deep breaths and close your eyes. Slowly imagine yourself walking down the ten steps of a staircase leading to your deeper structure. Ten, nine, eight. As you step down to reach your unconscious mind, you notice how every step brings you into a more relaxed state. Seven, six, five, four. As you approach from the last steps, you notice how everything feels so light, calm, clear and simple. Three, two, one. You are now in touch with your true self.

If you prefer to be guided by a live voice and just sit back, you can purchase the recordings of these activities on our website www. thinkyourselfseries.com. Either way it works. Trust yourself.

STEP ONE: HOW DO YOU PERCEIVE TIME?

If we ask you to point to an area of the room where your present is and where your future is, where would you point? Is your past behind you and your future in front of you? Or is your past to your left and your future to your right? If you were to make a line from your past to your future, where would the line be? Would it be from back to front or from left to right? And where is the present? Is the line going through you and you are standing in the present or is the line in front of you and you are looking at the line and seeing the past, the present and the future? Are you standing on the line? Which ever way you see it is perfect. There is no right or wrong. Knowing this just helps you visualize the steps of the exercise.

STEP TWO: NOTICING THE PRESENT.

From your fully relaxed sitting position, now physically stand up and invite your breathing to remain slow and stay into a state of comfort. Imagine time stretched out on the time line you have identified above. Standing in the present, turn to look at your past and see what brought you to become who you are today. Have you constantly been stressed out on a regular basis in the past? Have you tried to start a business and failed? Have you been applying for jobs without success? Now turn facing the future, and take a few steps into your future to realize how it will feel a year from now. If you don't change what you are doing right now, what will your future look like? How will it feel ? If you don't make any changes to the way you organize your days, and mostly, the way you think, will you continue to be stressed out? Will your business continue to think you are unable to start a business? Will you continue to experience failure when applying for jobs?

STEP THREE: NEGATIVE EMOTION RELEASE

Now, step back into the present. Imagine yourself stepping up above your body like an outer-body experience, and look down at your time line. Look down at your past, present and future. You can choose to place a thick sheet of plexiglass between yourself and your timeline so that past experiences will remain down in the past and you will only be an observer.

As you look at your past, you can see all those times when you had a bad experience. See every attempt at signing a new client that did not work; every time you looked at yourself in the mirror with a sensation of failure. And as you look down, from up above, you can realize that each of these experiences was a training ground for your future. Notice the information that emerges from each of these experiences. Remember that your brain can process information very fast. Trust your unconscious mind to stop at every instance where it feels that you have had an experience from which some negative emotions remained. Ask your unconscious mind to take only the positive learning from that experience and to release the negative emotion. All you ever needed from this experience was that positive learning. And now, with that positive learning, the negative emotion will go away.

Let the new information float out as a radiant glow. Take that light with you and keep it available so you can use it in the future. Everything else - negative emotions and limiting beliefs - can exit your body and be released from your past.

Come back from your past to the present, stopping at each event that has affected your successful journey, collecting the positive learning. Once back in the present, and once you have learned everything you need to acknowledge in order for the negative emotion to be released, open your eyes and feel how this new information will help you in the future. Notice how your future has now shifted and changed in light of that new learning.

STEP FOUR: SHIFT

Now close your eyes again and float way up in the air again. Look down at your timeline and see how your past looks different now. Realize that all those experiences were just generating results and that now, you feel good about them. Whatever troubled you has left and is getting further away by the second. As you feel good about your past, look down at your future and imagine the best kinds of feelings in it. Fill every future experience with the best state of mind. See your future looking better than ever.

STEP FIVE: EXPERIENCE THE FUTURE

Come back down through the plexiglass and slowly get back into your body. Feel full of excitement, anticipating the most amazing future. See yourself having the best success of your life. Experience a life full of the most wonderful things, new people, new possibilities, greater health, more money, new activities, new habits!

Now physically step forward on your line towards the future. Notice how your whole future has now shifted and changed from what you experienced in the first part of the exercise. Feel how it feels to be successful, to be exactly how you want to be, to feel how you want to feel, to hear others tell you how great you are and how amazing you are!

STEP SIX: NEW YOU

You can now open your eyes and feel the NEW YOU transformed and ready for a compelling and exciting future.

You won't stop having external pressure or challenges; you will simply be able to deal with them differently. In light of this new learning, you have now understood its purpose and how to release the negative emotions that accompany each learning experience. It doesn't mean that you will never have a negative emotion again; it means that if you go there, you won't stay there long. You now have the tools to get out of any problem. You can choose to use this negative emotion release process any time in your every day life.

KEY CONCEPTS

NEGATIVE EMOTION RELEASE

Although challenges are designed to teach us a lesson and make us grow, some experiences are causing us to create limiting beliefs and negative emotions. We can release these by acknowledging the positive learning that our life events brought to us.

CHAPTER 31

REPLACING NEGATIVE FEELINGS AND BEHAVIOURS

"I will form good habits and become their slave. And how will I accomplish this difficult feat? Through these scrolls it will be done, for each scroll contains a principle which will drive a bad habit from my life and replace it with one which will bring me closer to success." — *Og Mandino*

Neutralize the past. The technique we just did was an exercise that will have taken care of all your limiting beliefs in general. Mostly, everything that has generated negative emotions has been lifted and is now exiting your body. It allowed you to shift your previous negative emotions into positive learning from your experiences.

Here is another technique that you can use in order to neutralize very specific incidents that you feel have caused you to be stuck. There might be some specific experiences that, once disconnected from your past, will allow you to better move on. In fact, sometimes we remember a negative experience because of how it made us feel. The experience in itself was not negative. Our response to it is what we remember. A state cannot be erased. It can only be replaced by something else, a more serving one.

REPLACING A NEGATIVE FEELING

In this exercise, you will remember an experience that you classified as negative and replace the feeling that this experience generates by positive feelings.

STEP ONE: GETTING INTO THE REPLACEMENT STATE

Now, think of a time when you were feeling on top of the world. Immerse yourself in this situation. Let that fantastic sensation grow, imagine it moving through your entire body. Take this feeling, give it the colour of your choice and imagine it springing through your past so that it covers every negative memory and every bad experience. Imagine soaking them with this really great feeling.

STEP TWO: IDENTIFY THE NEGATIVE FEELING YOU WANT TO ERASE

Think abo t a part of your life when you felt stuck or blocked. Think of a moment that gives you bad feelings and limits your behaviour. Maybe an episode of your life when you forgot an important document that almost cost you your job or a time when someone you care about told you that you were inadequate.

STEP THREE: WHITE IT OUT

Imagine watching the negative experience on a giant screen. Imagine a brightness button on the side of the screen. In one quick move, turn it all the way to the maximum brightness, until you white it out completely. One moment you see it and the next, it is completely whited out. Do it again. Imagine it and white it out really quickly. Repeat 2 or 3 times until it comes naturally.

STEP FOUR: REPLACE THE STATE

Take the amazing feeling and as you imagine the difficult situation again, white out the negative feeling and spin this really good feeling in its place. Focus on the good feeling spinning fast in your body and notice the good feeling.

STEP FIVE: BACK TO NEUTRAL

Shake your body and go back to a neutral state.

STEP SIX: VERIFY THE PROCESS

To verify that this new strategy works out automatically, think about the negative situation and see how you are feeling. Can you imagine feeling badly? How does that make your feel? Repeat the process until you feel great when you think about the situation.

REPLACING A NEGATIVE BEHAVIOUR

You can also use the following similar exercise to achieve the same result with something you wish you were not doing anymore. This time, use a behaviour, instead of a feeling.

STEP ONE: GETTING INTO THE REPLACEMENT BEHAVIOUR

Think of the last time you did something amazing like having a fulfilled day at work, or accomplishing a lot, or having organized your schedule to take time for yourself. Get into the pride generated by doing the right thing and how amazing it felt.

STEP TWO: IDENTIFY THE BEHAVIOUR YOU WANT TO ERASE.

Think of the last time you did something that self-sabotaged your success. Think of something that still bothers you. Think of something you don't want to think about anymore. Think of the visual representation, the image or movie you see in your mind's eye.

STEP THREE: MAKE IT DISAPPEAR

Take a picture of the event and make it smaller. Move it far into the distance. Take the colour and the brightness out of it. If you hear voices and sounds of the scene, make them fade away. Make the picture so small that you have to squint to see it. Then make it even smaller. When it is the size of a breadcrumb, brush it away. Repeat the process three times.

STEP FOUR: REPLACE THE STATE

As you make the image disappear, get into your replacement state and fully immerse yourself into the desired behaviour that you want instead.

STEP FIVE: RETURN TO NEUTRAL

Shake your body and go back to a neutral state.

STEP SIX: TEST

Think about the situation that used to generate a negative behaviour and notice if your first thought is not to do the positive behaviour instead. Repeat the process as many times as you need in order to make this happen naturally.

When you think about past experiences, bad habits or things you shouldn't do, make sure the image looks like a white Polaroid. Push it off into the distance.

KEY CONCEPTS

NEUTRALIZE THE PAST

Experiences in life are neither positive nor negative. The way we respond to these experiences are making them good or bad. If a specific event causes us to have negative emotions, we can change the negative feeling by a more desired one.

Responses cannot be deleted; they can only be replaced. When a specific event causes us grief, we can change our response to the event by replacing it with a different behaviour.

CHAPTER 32

NEGATIVE TO POSITIVE

"Train your mind to see the positive. You will find what you are looking for." — *Unknown*

Now that you know how to clear of negative emotions and negative behaviours, you are ready to turn Negative into Positive. We have learned in the neurological levels section how the beliefs and values are crucial and how they can affect our behaviours. The problem occurs when these beliefs are negative. We call them limiting beliefs.

The questions below are part of a process that will open up the boundaries of your unconscious limits. When you are in a problem box, sometimes you don't even realize it. This exercise will create windows and open up the walls so that you can see outside the box. The realizations that will occur as your walls go down will generate the light bulbs in your head in order for you to get the motivation you need to let go of the old beliefs. It will make you recognize that these beliefs that you thought were part of your life, are only true in your head and are not serving you. Therefore, they must go.

We will learn in this section how to turn them from negative to positive using our linguistic. The power of words is very strong. You can actually breakdown any problem linguistically. As you will learn how your words impact your behaviours, you will start noticing your thoughts and you will be able to mentally hit the Cancel button whenever you get a negative thought. You will catch yourself having a negative thought and replacing it with a good thought.

It starts right now with the most frequently asked question. When people ask you: "How are you doing?" create your own response. Use your words to create your situation. Pretend. Think about it wisely next time you are about to respond: "I'm okay, thank you." *Okay*? That's it? That is your total aspiration? You just told your brain that you want to be only *okay*. Not more? What will happen if you take this opportunity and every time someone asks you how you're doing, you say instead: "I am great", "I am awesome", "I am fantastic"? It would be serving you a lot more to program your brain to be amazing!

How about the anticipation of a feeling? Something that is not happening yet, but that we plan ahead to feel badly. Nathalie once asked a participant in her class the Million Dollar question: *How are you?* Nathalie tells us the story.

"When I asked her "How are you", she said: "I am tired! Well, I am not tired now but I will be by the end of the day. I have so much to do and I have to pick up the kids after work and take one to soccer, one to guitar lessons and I will probably get stuck in traffic and get pissed off." So I asked: "Are you tired now?" She said: "No, not yet." "Are you in traffic now?" I asked. She said: "No not yet." So, I said: "Why are you already programming yourself to be tired? Why aren't you saying instead: "I will feel so great tonight because I will have accomplished so much in my day. I will take advantage of the traffic to catch up on my audio book to which I have been listening. It will be awesome! Also, while my son is at soccer, I will drop my daughter to guitar and take 20 minutes to go for a short run to energize myself before I pick them up again at the end of their sessions.""

Do you have a global positioning system? A GPS? When you get off track and decide to turn when it is not time, what does the GPS say?

Recalculating! So that is what we would like you to do every time you get off track. When you hear yourself say, 'I am so stupid!', quickly hear yourself say, 'Oh, wait, what did I just think? *recalculating*. I just said something stupid. I am really intelligent and I probably did not think much before saying this. I am willing to pay more attention from now on so that I can say intelligent things.'

Here is your chance to start to *recalculate* more of your thoughts. The next series of questions will bring more digging to find out what has been keeping you from reaching your goals. What beliefs do you hold that could be transformed to serve you better? You know the nasty voice you hear in your head? We are the result of what we think and what we have been thinking our entire life.

Ask yourself how does the idea of success make you feel? Your personal assistant wants to make you right. So be very careful what you want to be right about. We can choose what we do and what we think. We can make it fabulous. Listen to your own internal dialogue which tells you about your own beliefs.

How do you feel about success?

Example: "I am afraid that being successful means that I have to give something up."

_____

_____

_____

What is your belief about it? Does it have to be hard?

Example: "I believe that success cannot happen without hard work and an excruciating amount of long nights working late."

_____

_____

How can you change this belief?

Example: "With a bit of planning and organization, I can choose a schedule that allows me to keep everything and be successful, along with spending my evenings with my family."

Do you believe you'll ever be successful?

Example: "I have been dreaming about success for so long that I think I am now used to success being a dream and not something concrete."

How can you change this belief?

Example: "I am willing to re-program my belief so that I can break down my big dream into realistic and concrete steps towards achieving it."

How would you rather feel and believe about success?

Example: "I feel like success belongs to me." "It is within my reach." "I am worth living my dream and I am turning it into reality."

In light of the answers to these few questions about your beliefs around success, you are now realizing how your own language and the way you think has been creating your own model of reality. It is like you were programming yourself to be disappointed.

Disappointment requires lots of planning. If we begin to look at things as if they are difficult, they will be. If we study what makes things impossible, we will find out. We plan way in advance to be disappointed. If we think something will be hard and strenuous, it will be. It is setting us up for failure. If we are doing something and it is not working, there has to be an easier way. We have to do something else. And the first thing we have to do is to change our internal state. It begins with our thoughts, and thoughts become actions and actions become habits and habits become beliefs and beliefs become who we truly are.

Now you know that you have a choice. Continue to believe these limiting beliefs or change the way you see the whole thing. We will invite you to re-write your beliefs, choosing to turn them into something that will serve you better.

USE YOUR SENSES TO RE-WRITE LIMITING BELIEFS

There are many ways to enhance your language. Use your senses when you re-phrase them. Make it happen in your head with visual, auditory and feelings. What will happen when you start believing these things? You're going to *see* yourself getting up feeling rested and refreshed in the morning. You will *hear* yourself talking with confidence with a new prospect client. You will *see* yourself taking time to enjoy yourself with your kids and friends. You will *hear* the voice inside your head telling you how great it is to be loving what you do and to *feel* excited about getting at it in the morning, *being excited* about work. You will *trust* that you have this. That you are awesome! How are you going to *feel* when you can say "*I love my job*"? Sentences that include senses and emotions are very powerful.

Here are the limiting beliefs that we have identified in the Neurological Section of this book when we talked about BELIEFS & VALUES. Let's have a second look at them and see how they can be re-phrased.

Being successful is hard.

Depending on where you are with your mind shifting, you can re-phrase from one extreme to the other. You could choose to re-phrase this way:

> *Example Re-phrase: "BEING SUCCESSFUL IS EASY."*
>
> *Which may be really pushing it depending on where you are at this time. You may want to choose a more transitional language like:*
>
> *Example Re-phrase: "I AM LEARNING HOW IT FEELS TO BE SUCCESSFUL."*
>
> *"This time it will be different. I know I used to think that way and that is the reason why I thought it was hard because I had chosen to think it was. Now that I am seeing it as easy, I will succeed easily."*

When you start making more money, you spend more, and you always stay in a position where you live paycheque to paycheque.

Example Re-phrase: WHEN YOU START MAKING MORE MONEY, YOU ALWAYS HAVE MONEY IN THE BANK AND YOUR SAVINGS ACCOUNT GROWS BIGGER ALL THE TIME. YOU ALWAYS HAVE MORE THAN ENOUGH MONEY TO PAY ALL YOUR BILLS AND MORE.

This new way of thinking is permanent and money is a great thing that generates great feelings (as opposed to creating discomfort every time you think about it).

In my family, we were told that working is boring but we all need a job.

Example Re-phrase: THE WAY I OCCUPY MY DAYS IS FULFILLING AND I LOVE WHAT I DO. I LOVE MY JOB AND I AM HAPPY GOING TO WORK EVERYDAY.

That is how I am; I am doomed to stay this way.

Example Re-phrase: THAT IS HOW I USED TO BE, NOW I AM BECOMING WHAT I REALLY WANT TO BE. I AM LEARNING HOW IT FEELS TO BE SUCCESSFUL.

No matter how hard I work or what I do, I can't get on top of things.

Example Re-phrase: I AM GETTING GREAT AT PLANNING MY SCHEDULE SO THAT I GET ON TOP OF THINGS AND I FINISH EACH DAY FEELING LIKE I HAVE ACCOMPLISHED ALL OF THE IMPORTANT THINGS I NEEDED TO DO. I EVEN HAVE TIME FOR PERSONAL STUFF.

I don't have willpower so I can't succeed.

Example Re-phrase: I   BELIEVE   THAT   I   HAVE EVERYTHING I NEED TO SUCCEED.

I cannot live without my tv shows.

Example Re-phrase: I ORGANIZE MY SCHEDULE WELL SO   THAT   I   EVEN   HAVE   TIME   TO   WATCH   MY FAVOURITE TV SHOW.

Being successful is a lot of work.

Example Re-phrase: I DO WORK TO BE SUCCESSFUL AND I AM LOVING IT. BEING SUCCESSFUL IS FUN! I AM ENJOYING THE PROCESS. BEING SUCCESSFUL GETS EASIER AND EASIER.

Planning is hard and gives me headaches.

Example Re-phrase: I AM GETTING GREAT AT PLANNING AND IT IS BECOMING MORE AND MORE NATURAL.

I have children so I cannot be successful.

Example Re-phrase: I HAVE CHILDREN SO I HAVE A GREAT REASON TO BE SUCCESSFUL, THEY GIVE ME THE DRIVE I NEED AND THEY ARE HELPING TO MAKE MY LIFE COMPLETE.

It's your turn now. You have read lots of examples and you are ready.

List the things that you hear yourself say that are self-limiting:

Example: "I am a failure" "I will probably screw up again." "I have a money problem." "I don't know what to do." "I'm always tired." "I am stressed all the time." "I can never finish anything!" "I never have time for myself!"

1. _____

2. _____

3. _____

4. _____

5. _____

Use your linguistic (words) to re-phrase your limiting beliefs.

Re-write them in a way that they can serve you. What should you chose to believe instead? How can you rephrase these to motivate yourself?

In order to help you with this exercise, here are some questions you can ask yourself in order to lower the intensity of the problems.

How? What? When? Where? And who specifically? (Do not ask why)

Says who? According to whom? Everybody?

Always? Never?

Nobody? Nothing? All? No one?

Compared to whom? Compared to what?

How do you know? What stops you? What would happen if you could?

What would happen if you did? What would happen if you didn't?

Go ahead. Turn the negative above into positive below:

> *Example: "I am in the right mindset." "When I get to the office today..."*
> *"It's easy to succeed." "I am learning how it feels to love selling." "I stay*
> *away from distractions very easily." "I plan time to exercise." "My schedule*
> *is getting lighter." "I am a great manager." "I am reaching my goals." "I*
> *am releasing unwanted habits." "I am increasing my confidence." "I am*
> *enhancing my ability to grow." "I am achieving my goal."*

1. _____

2. _____

3. _____

4. _____

5. _____

Once you have written them, repeat them as often as you can until they start becoming a part of you. These new beliefs are to be carried with your well-formed outcome. There are only five here. You will want to pay very close attention to your thoughts and soon, you will be amazed at how easy it is to turn a limiting belief into a positive statement that will serve you.

You will become a professional beliefs transformer. Watch your life go from a negative to a positive trend.

KEY CONCEPTS

NEGATIVE TO POSITIVE

Our lack of success may have led us to create some limiting beliefs regarding success.

As these beliefs dictate the way we act, we might as well change them in order for these beliefs to support our desires as opposed to standing in the way of realizing that for which we aim.

You can start changing a belief by linguistically re-phrasing it.

PART 7:

THE "A"

CHAPTER 33

ACTUALIZE - RE-DEFINE

"And Suddenly you know it is time for a new beginning."
— *Meister Eckhart*

The third component of the D.N.A. System is the ACTUALIZE section. Now that you have cleaned out your old negative emotions and limiting beliefs, you will learn how to install the new desires you came up with in the first section. Techniques of anchoring, alternating behaviours, assuming excellence and taking action will guide you into programming the NEW YOU.

The ACTUALIZE section will help you to re-define the choices you will continue to make once your new desires are installed. This section will also prepare you for alternative choices in the event you face unexpected situations. You will learn how to become accountable to yourself and feel authentic by daily feeding your brain.

You have elicited your DESIRE and created a NEW YOU. You are now ready to install the desires and program your brain with what you want. This section will teach you how to implement and cement your desires. You have chosen your new kitchen, you know exactly what you want, you got rid of the old cupboards and now it is time to install the new ones and lay down the new marble counter top.

This section will not only allow you to get a strong new foundation for your new successful life, it will also ensure that you have the tools to get to the best you want to be and maintain your New You so that the emotions of failure don't come back.

You can use each of these processes separately. We suggest you do them one by one and take some time to implement each new achieved state before moving on to the next exercise.

KEY CONCEPTS

ACTUALIZE

The third component of the D.N.A. System is the ACTUALIZE part. You will learn in this section how to implement and program your desires into your brain.

CHAPTER 34

IDENTITY - INTEGRATION AND SYNTHESIS OF OUR TRUE SOURCE

"I think every person has their own identity and beauty. Everyone being different is what is really beautiful. If we were all the same, it would be boring." — Tila Tequila

The next neurological level is Identity. At this level, we integrate and synthesize our true source. All the knowledge you have accumulated so far in your journey through the four previous levels is contributing to create who you are. YOU.

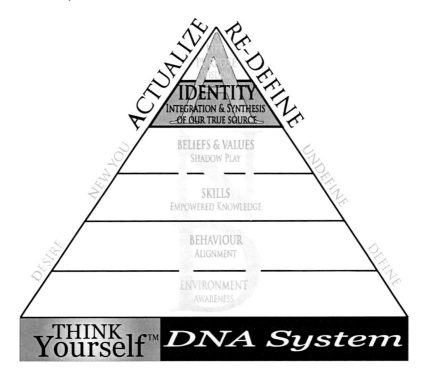

When you start to actualize, you are moving from a greater place of integration and synthesis. You are in greater alignment, and your life reflects that alignment. Your behaviours are in line with your beliefs and values, which allows you to use your skills in an environment that support your identity. You are the result of all of these levels combined. What you manifest externally represents your truest desire as you now know yourself and what you want. Life becomes more joyful and the act of co-creation is playful and easy.

> *"All movement is generated from my power centre. I am free to express myself, knowing where my true source lies."* — Tasha Hughes

In this section, we will help you determine your identity. The big 'I am'. The following section will help clarify and anchor your next direction. The questions in the tool below are marked by a greater sense of lightness and ease as integration and synthesis occurs.

Who am I?

> *Example: "I am a mother and I am successful in my job. I work hard so that I am able to provide my children with a good life and I am an inspiration to them so that they, in turn, will reach their best self."*

_____

_____

What do I love about the answer to that question?

> *Example: "I love how empowered I feel to create a good life for me and my family."*

_____

_____

Is there anything that I do not like about how I answered that question? Is part of 'me' missing, lost, or as of yet unexplored?

Example: "I would rather work in my own business and not so hard"

"Who am I to be Brilliant? Gorgeous? Talented? The Real question is: Who am I NOT to be? - Marianne Williamson

Who am I NOW?

Example: "I am a mother and I am successful in my own business and it's fun and easy. I am able to provide my children with a good life and I am spending lots of time with them. I am an inspiration to them so that they, in turn, will reach their best self."

Who AM I when I am having fun?

Example: "I am a friend, a mother, a sister, a work-colleague, a team-mate"

When do you feel that your environment, behaviours, skills, beliefs and values are integrated?

Example: "When I do something that I am good at, in an environment that supports what is important to me, is when I feel that my identity is integrated."

When you are feeling challenged, with what part of your identity are you negotiating?

Example: "When I am deep in the middle of a work project - in the zone - I find it challenging to be interrupted by my children who want to spend time with me. I don't know who to choose? Me, the successful entrepreneur or me, the loving mother."

When do you feel that two parts of your identity are colliding?

Example: "At work, I had been trying to arrange a meeting with my boss to discuss my raise. He finally called me into his office just as I was leaving for a personal engagement that was important to me. I found myself torn between my professional me and my personal me."

Which of my identities do I want to be more of, or can I merge both identities so that I don't have to choose?

Example: "I realize that the mom part of me and the business-woman part of me both want the same thing for me – they both want me to be happy. I now realize that I don't have to choose, I can keep both and use them to my advantage and I can even use the mom at work and the business woman at home and enjoy having each identity as a tool in my arsenal.

What would that look like?

Example: "At work, when I am training an associate on a task, I am more nurturing and patient like I would be at home as a mom." "At home, I can apply my assertiveness and negotiating skills with my family using my confident business me."

Now let's go back to the outcome you elicited in chapter twenty-five. If you were to achieve your outcome, would that be in line with your personality, your family system and your overall values? Does that fit with who you are? Are you five foot tall wanting to become a professional basketball player? Or do you have the shape of a football player with strong athletic features and want to weigh less than a hundred pounds? If, in order to get to your goal, for example, you had to leave town for three years and not see your children and family. Would that be acceptable to you?. Respond honestly to the question.

Does your outcome fit with your identity?

Example: "The outcome I elicited earlier was mainly written to fit with my business-me. I will now make sure to add a sentence about how easy it is to integrate other facets of my identity to my outcome: "My life is complete as I am free to be every part of myself simultaneously."

KEY CONCEPTS

INTEGRATION & SYNTHESIS

The answers to these questions will allow you to combine everything you have learned so far, integrate and synthesize this knowledge in order to find your identity.

The integration of all parts of yourself allows you to stop fighting with your own self and start embracing fully each part and live true to your complete identity.

CHAPTER 35

SELF-CARE - BACK TO BASICS

"The goal is to create space where you were once stuck. To unveil layers of protection you've built around your heart. To appreciate your body and become aware of the mind and the noise it creates. To make peace with who you are. The goal is to love, ...well, you." — *Rachel Brathen on The Goal of Yoga*

Now that you are clear about you who are, we are introducing you to an easy technique to protect and preserve your newly found identity. In order to be successful and have the vitality needed to ACTUALIZE our positive outcome, we need to commit first and foremost to our own self-care. Your identity is not only internal. Your physical body is also part of who you are.

When hearing the name of Nathalie's first book of the series: *THINK Yourself*™ *THIN* for the first time, a lot of people thought: "Alright, I don't have to do anything, no exercise, no eating healthy, I just have to think and magic will happen!" In reading the book and discovering the system, they soon found out that this book is far from being a book about not doing anything. It is about programming you to actually be *doing* it instead of just *knowing* you should do it.

It is the same for THINK Yourself™ SUCCESSFUL. Success is whole. It is not just about the mind. The body is certainly a huge part of your success. It is the vehicle that will drive you through success.

Self-care is nourishment, and proper nourishment leads to a state of thriving. It is therefore imperative that we be mindful of the influences we allow into our lives. You will agree by now that this book is certainly

more about the mind than it is about the body. However, a healthy body is imperative and inherent to any type of success. Which immensely rich, successful... and sick woman would not give all her fortune to get her health back?

How and what we eat and drink, who we spend time with both personally and professionally, the books we read, music we listen to, thoughts we engage in, the stories we tell ourselves, are all things we consume. They all become part of our internal landscape. Our internal landscape needs to produce fertile soil, and the best conditions in which to cultivate our external reality.

Nathalie, Mo and Tasha all realize the absolute importance of a healthy body in order to produce the best mind possible. In order to reap the most benefit from the material in this book, in the least amount of time, the body as well as the mind needs to be enlisted. Rather than viewing it as a chore, just in case you do, view it as an opportunity for self-care. Commitment to self-care equals commitment to your own identity.

Yoga, or stretching, is a perfect metaphor for this. When we stretch, we become aware of areas in our bodies where we experience restriction. We notice where we feel tight, how we feel limited, where we need to place our attention to create a greater sense of freedom. So self-care becomes a fantastic tool for greater self-awareness. With greater self-awareness we see where we need to go to create greater success.

Here are seven strategies you can use for self-care.

FOOD

Proper nutrition. What we consume, we become. As a general rule, ask yourself if you know from where the food comes. Eat whole food, transformed as little as possible, mostly plant-based and not too much of it. Eat a rainbow of food. Blue is your water, and your plate should be filled with all of the other vibrant colours. It is in these colours that vital antioxidants are found. Beets, dark leafy vegetables, sweet potatoes, coloured peppers. Half of your plate should be vegetables, a quarter should be protein and the last quarter can be a starch. i.e. sweet potatoes, quinoa. Avoid the whites, (i.e. flour, sugar, potatoes, pasta) and stay away from packaged foods. Include healthy fats which are crucial to keeping your brain happy along with seven other systems of your body. They will make your hair shine, your skin glow, lower your cholesterol, keep your heart healthy, etc., for example, extra virgin olive oil, avocados and nuts. These are just a few suggestions on food. For more, stay tuned for the next book of the series: *THINK Yourself™ CLEAN from the inside out*.

MOVEMENT

Your favourite way to move your body. For some it is a run, a spin class, yoga, or even just putting on your favourite music to dance! Just move in ways that make you feel vital (yes, sex counts!).

Movement sends fresh new energy to the brain so that it can process and retain information faster and better. Therefore, you will experience optimal gains from this book if you intentionally move your body either before, or after, tackling sections of this book. It will enhance your experience, clear out the cobwebs, and help to create a clean slate.

SLEEP

Sleep when you need it. It is not the quantity of sleep, it is the quality of it. Nothing will bolster your creativity, immune system and productivity more. No guilt required. The body knows what it needs to function optimally. Let your body decide when it is time to get up, not your alarm clock. You can avoid time wasted trying to fall asleep by using your personal assistant. Just place an order every night as soon as you lay your head on the pillow. Say to yourself: "While I fall into a deep and comfortable sleep in a few minutes, I would like you to do all my thinking and have some answers for me when I wake up refreshed tomorrow morning." This will make sure you trust your unconscious mind to deliver in the morning and let you get a full restful sleep. Your personal assistant and your chef know the answers to your questions and know everything about your schedule and your to-do list. Let them do the work while you recharge.

SAY YES

Say YES …..to new opportunities, things that scare you, situations that support you, anything that makes you curious. You will then be better able to create a successful life, *by design*, not by default.

SAY NO

Say NO … to those people and situations that no longer serve you. Recognize when you need to pull back in order to take care of yourself. Say no to things that stand in the way of having space and energy to focus on the things you want.

> *"If it is not a Hell Yes! Then it is a no."*
> — *Nathalie Plamondon-Thomas*

ASK AND RECEIVE

ASK and Receive … for what you need. 'Receiving' is a hurdle for many women because we are so good at giving. We can also question our own 'worthiness' and find receiving uncomfortable. We cannot be successful if we do not first practice receiving. Be mindful of the many small opportunities in any given day that we have to learn how to both ask for and receive that of which we want more.

USE THE D.N.A. SYSTEM

Use the tools of this book! There are so many layers that can be applied to every area of your life. Almost magically, when you focus the tools of this book on one area of your life, it will influence your way of thinking, feeling and seeing yourself and the world around you. That can only impact other areas of your life in a positive way, until you can intentionally refocus your efforts in the next area of your life!

KEY CONCEPTS

SELF-CARE

Proper nutrition, movement, sleep, saying yes and saying no, asking, receiving and using the tools in this book will allow you to care for yourself.

CHAPTER 36

LIFE PURPOSE - WISDOM

"The power you have is to be the best version of yourself you can be, so you can create a better world." ~ *Ashley Rickards*

The last level of the pyramid is Life Purpose, Wisdom and Leadership.

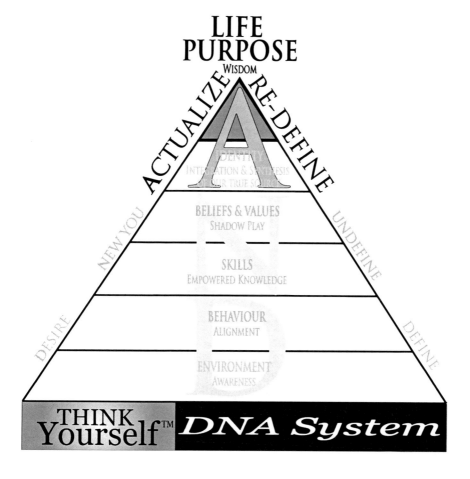

LEAD WITH YOUR 'WHY'

Now that you have answered several very important questions about your environment, your behaviours, your skills, your beliefs and values, you have opened your mind. You now have access to most of the pieces of the puzzle. Nathalie's friend Kelly makes puzzles all the time. Kelly has a process, a system. She starts by looking at the picture on the cover and noticing the big picture she is getting to, ahead of time. She observes the edges, the top and the bottom, the details and each area of the final image. Then she starts taking pieces out of the box. First, she picks only the ones with a flat edge. They would be the ones that would consist of making the frame, the outside of the puzzle. Then once the rim has been built, she takes more pieces out and selects those with similar colours and puts them together. Each step gets her closer to the final picture. Answering the questions of this book are steps and layers that are being installed in your brain. Each question brings you closer to your goal.

The image is really starting to come together, you have made some associations, putting all the pieces together... you have created the edges and then filled in most of the picture, and now you are down to the very last few pieces that will make the image clear and brilliant, the middle, the heart, the core of it all is coming now...

Michelangelo believed that in every piece of marble, the image already exists, the art is already there, all we have to do is to reveal it. All this time you had it inside of you. The reason you are doing everything you do is at the core, the heart of it all. It is your life purpose. It is like you had the answers all along at the bottom of a drawer but somehow, there was so much non-useful stuff accumulated in the drawer that you could no longer see the bottom, where clarity and wisdom reside.

Answering a WHY question might have been challenging at the beginning of the book when we first asked you back in chapter 22. Now that you have all of the pieces of the puzzle, you know what you want and what is important to you, you have cleared your limiting beliefs and negative emotions and you know who you are, you will find that answers will come to you naturally.

Now we need to elicit and take out of the box all the main pieces of the puzzle that represent your 'why'. Taking out of the box the reasons why you want what you want. We know you have more   than likely done this millions of times. You may even be tired of promising yourself, once again, that this will be the year that things finally turn out well for you. It is about feeling great about yourself and not about what others could think or want you to do. It is about YOU first.

Once we live life from a greater place of integration and alignment, we naturally move into a place of leadership and wisdom. These next questions will further open up your unconscious mind to move you closer to self-mastery. Self-Mastery leads to purpose and our highest calling.

Why do you want the things you want?

Example: "I want the things that I want because I feel it is my calling."

_____

_____

What do you love?

Example: "I love making people grow and realize their full potential."

Who do you love?

Example: "I love my children, I love my family and I love people that know me from the inside out and like me anyway." "I love people because I want to love them. I love the love that I give more than the love I receive."

What brings you joy? Sense of Purpose? Peace?

Example: "My children", "helping others", "creating something new", "acknowledging someone else's goodness".

What do you know for sure? And what is your 'Big Why'?

Example: "I know for sure ... that I have a perspective on life and gifts to offer that no one else on this planet has in quite the same way. I know that I am unique, which in no way diminishes the person next to me. They are also unique." "My BIG WHY is to create the legacy of a better world for my children, where they can more easily live their own gifts, and find joy in helping others."

What is your perfect life?

Example: "My perfect life is living my life purpose in my everyday actions, using my skills and being in line with what I believe and what is important to me. All of this, in an environment that supports me." "I wake up every morning filled with a sense of joy, purpose, meaning and choices that I have created."

How does that reinvention make you FEEL?

Example: "It makes me feel like I am in charge of my own life."

How do you feel free now?

Example: "I feel free now because what I was simply hoping for in the past, is now clearly within my reach. Faith has replaced hope."

Life purpose is all about what is beyond you. It is your own unique life path within the context of serving someone else other than yourself. Beyond your identity, who else are you serving?

How are you a contributor?

Example: "I contribute by living my true life purpose which helps those around me and gives other people permission to do the same."

Now that you have tapped into all six layers of your brain, let's go back to chapter 25 where you wrote your positive outcome. Now that you are familiar with each level, you can expand your outcome a bit more. Use the next exercise to give more substance to your goal.

Project yourself in the future. Pretend you have achieved your goal. What does your environment look like? How far from home do your work? What are the tasks you are doing? What are you good at? What feelings exactly are you going to feel? What will people tell you? What will you tell yourself when you wake up in the morning? What will be present in your life that is currently missing? Beyond the bank account, what else is there to gain with your success? What is the intention behind the behaviour? Visualize yourself being successful. What does that do for you? Does it empower you, does it give you self-confidence, and does it give you energy? What does it do?

Re-write your positive outcome:

> *Example: "I get up in the morning rested after a long night's sleep and I am excited about my day. I feel that I am using my skills and what I am good at in my everyday tasks, and work in an environment with positive people, and have the resources I need. I feel that what I am doing fits with my values and what is important to me, and that I can be myself and feel at ease and comfortable with what I do. Moreover, I feel that I contribute to the world as I am achieving my life purpose and I am my very best self."*

_____

_____

You will now continue your journey in the ACTUALIZE section and complete the D.N.A. System with tools, techniques, success tips and... to fully immerse yourself into your new found identity and live your life's purpose. Acquiring the knowledge is one thing. Now we will teach you how to maintain it and ACTUALIZE it in your whole life.

KEY CONCEPTS

WISDOM & LEADERSHIP

Finding our life's purpose allows us to step higher than our own self. Finding wisdom is to step into our leader's shoes and ask ourselves: "Who else am I serving?"

Beyond being the best we can be, beyond our own identity, to whom or what can we contribute?

CHAPTER 37

RE-INVENT YOUR DAILY LIFE

"No problem can be solved from the same level of consciousness that cre-ated it." — *Albert Einstein*

Exploring the DNA System, you have gone through a journey of shifting a negative mindset to a positive one, from limiting beliefs to more expanded ones. You have shifted your self-awareness and found a new identity and purpose for yourself. You can now design a new life in which your wildest dreams will become reality. This new reality doesn't mean that you will never face any challenges from now on. It means that you are now equipped to problem solve from a different level of consciousness.

In this chapter, we are offering you a simple linguistic tool that you can use anytime you go through a decision-making process or face a challenge. You can re-invent your daily life with powerful words in your arsenal. This chapter is providing you with the groundwork. Think of a problem you are trying to solve. Allow your mind to consider the following words and ideas in relation to the problem you are trying to solve. Write the word that compels you the most at the top of the page. Now do some free-form writing about the problem/solution through the lens of that word. Repeat with other words until inspiration happens!!

Solutions can take many forms, and often the unconscious mind will work in pictures, so be aware of this level of consciousness communicating through non-verbal means such as memories, symbols, pictures, or any of the senses. Don't second guess yourself. Trust that your subconscious mind knows and has a story to tell. Then follow the trail!

POWERFUL "RE" WORDS:

Remember	Re-program
ReDEFINE	Re-engage
Recalibrate	Re-organize
Recover	Re-prioritize
Re-energize	RE-INVENT

Sometimes the solution to any problem lies in the problem itself.

"The magic is in the mess." — *Brene Brown*

When considering a problem, sometimes a completely clean slate is required. Other times, revisiting and refreshing previously shelved or forgotten ideas or talents can lead to something wonderful.

Example: I love being a Mom. However, I have become very accustomed to throwing on "Mom" clothes, hair in ponytail, and heading out the door. Even my professional clothes have become 'comfy' and easy. Honestly, it makes me feel frumpy. I want to re-invent and re-energize my wardrobe, my image, and my hair. I am going to first collect images from magazines and Pinterest of how I want to look and feel. Then I am going to hire an Image Consultant who will help we recycle some of what I already own, and help me decide which looks work best for me now.

Your turn, think of the challenge you have and re-invent it:

_____

_____

_____

_____

KEY CONCEPTS

FROM PROBLEM TO SOLUTION

You can linguistically talk yourself out of a problem by using Re-words to transform the state you are in.

CHAPTER 38

ACT & MERGE

"The secret of having it all is believing you already do." — *unknown*

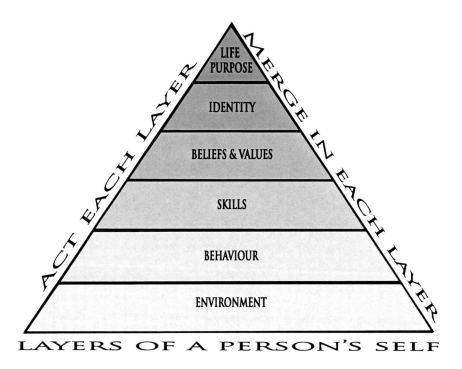

LAYERS OF A PERSON'S SELF

Act. Action is imperative to actualizing a New You. It is not enough to read and reflect. Real and lasting change requires that we move outside of our comfort zone. Action is the tool to do exactly that! Sometimes we can get caught up in "analysis paralysis", or a relationship with perfectionism that leads to procrastination. In order to actualize, we need to stop thinking and just start doing.

Throughout the DNA System, you have learned that your identity is built with different layers. This exercise will place you in each neurological level in order for you to break down every level of yourself and assign a new reality to each part of you. You will assume a new environment, a new behaviour, new skills, news beliefs and values, new identity and new life purpose.

You will use the neurological levels to take action and figure out what you need in order to do or achieve your vision. We will invite you to make a list of what you need to be or have in order for your desired outcome to actualize.

As an example, some countries have analyzed and tried to copy Michael Phelp's swimming techniques. They first looked at his environment. What type of water does he train in? What is the temperature of this water? What fabric is his swimwear made of? Then they looked at his behaviours. How does he perform each stroke. Exactly when does his hand get immersed in the water? Which finger touches first? How does he stand just before jumping in the water? They also copied his skills. What is he really good at? Is it when he turns at the extremity of the pool? When does he get the lead? Is it in the first half or the second half? What does he do extremely well that differentiate him from his competition?

Now, unfortunately for the other countries, their "spying" techniques stopped there. They did not go beyond the first three layers of the brain. They did not know what Michael Phelps had INSIDE his head. What is he thinking when he trains? What is important to him? What does he value? What is in his head just before a race? What does he believe? What is his identity? When he responds to the question: "Who am I?" He more likely responds: "I am the fastest swimmer in the world." And what is his life purpose? Who else is he serving? Does he inspire young athletes? Maybe. We have to ask all these questions in order to be able to really get to all layers of the mind and install a new great serving habit.

Nathalie very often asks questions to her clients and they respond that they don't know the answers. Then she asks: "If you knew, what would that be?" Sometimes this question works, sometimes, there is still no answer. Then she asks: " What advice would you give someone in your situation?" Sometime that generates an answer and sometime, nothing comes up. So, then, she asks the magic questions: "Do you know someone who has been successful at this and what would they do in your situation?" All of a sudden, the responses are flowing. They say: "Well, they would certainly do such and such, etc." It is very funny how, once they put themselves in someone else's shoes, they have all the answers. They know exactly what someone else would do. Yet, the other person did not tell them what they did or have done or would do. The answers were inside the client's head. They just did not think they had them. You too, have everything you need inside. So go ahead. Ask yourself the questions.

"You have what it takes to be a victorious, independent, fearless woman."
~ Tyra Banks

First, respond to these questions to start awakening yourself to the concepts of the questions.

What is the environment of successful people? Where are they? Who is with them? Where do they hang out?

Example: "They must be surrounded with positive people." "They live in a nice clean house." "Their desk is organized." "They hang out with other successful people and genuine friends." "They hang out at the gym."

_____

_____

What are the behaviours of successful people? What do they do? What are their actions?

Example: "They are making prospect calls." "They are posting regularly on social media." "They are meeting lots of people."

_____

_____

What are the skills of successful people? What are they good at?

Example: "They are good at planning and organizing." "They are disciplined." "They are great at selling their services."

_____

_____

What are the beliefs and values of successful people? What do they believe? What is important to them?

Example: "They believe in themselves." "They believe they can do anything." "Their achievements are important to them." "They care about those closest to them."

_____

_____

Who are they? When they say: "I am..." fill in the blank

Example: "I am successful" "I am confident" "I am smart" "I am driven"

_____

_____

What is their life purpose? Who else are they serving?

Example: "They must be surrounded with positive people." "They live in a nice clean house." "Their desk is organized." "They hang out with other successful people and genuine friends." "They hang out at the gym."

_____

_____

ACT

Now that you have a few answers on paper, you can try it on in your head. As you know by now, your unconscious mind can process so much more information than what you are able to write down. You will stand up for this exercise and immerse yourself in each of these neurological levels to adopt them as your own.

Step one: Recall your desired outcome.

Go back to your desired outcome that we elicited in chapter 25. Fully immerse yourself in the outcome. Go there in your mind as if it was happening right now.

Step two: Imagine someone to model.

Now as you are thinking about your outcome, step into the shoes of someone that has already achieved this outcome. Maybe it is you, ten years ago, when you had your Mojo. Maybe you know someone you can model. Maybe you want to model a successful celebrity that seems to be how you want to be. You can also make a mental image of someone fictional that has achieved your desired outcome.

Step three: Environment

Imagine that our six levels pyramid is on the floor in front on you. You can also imagine six squares laid-out like a ladder on the floor. The first level, the closest to you says: Environment. Step into this first square. Close your eyes and ask yourself what is the environment for the people that have achieved your desired outcome? Where are the successful people? When are they? Withwhom? What is their environment? For example, you could think of places like their office. You can see them in their car. You can see them at the gym with other people that believe that exercise is connected to success. You can see what clothes they have in their closet. See all the places where the successful people hang out and all their material possessions.

For each square, take the time to see everything you need to see, hear and feel.

Step four: behaviours

Open your eyes and now step into the next square and pretend it is labeled: Behaviours. As you close your eyes again, ask yourself what do the successful people do in that environment? See everything that would be part of their behaviour. Organizing their schedule, planning their days, being focused at work, or whatever comes to your mind when you ask yourself what successful people do. Again, take the time to go through each behaviour or action that you suspect successful people do in those places.

Step five: Skills

The next square is called: Skills. Open your eyes for a second in order to step into it. What are the capabilities that successful people have in order to be able to do these behaviours in these places? What skills do they have? What is required in order to be able to succeed? Do they have knowledge of business? Are they good at planning? Selling? Are they good at fitting their personal time in? Are they good at going to bed early? Are they organized?

Step six: Beliefs and values

Open your eyes and step into the next square labeled: Beliefs and Values. What beliefs guide successful people? What do they believe about themselves that allows them to be successful? What is important to successful people? What do they value? Do they value success? Do they believe that their self is set at a successful version of themselves and that, no matter how, their behaviours will always guide them to go back to this set truth about what they are supposed to feel like and be like? Is balance important to them? Do they believe that taking the time to prepare is worth the few minutes in the morning? Are they self-confident? Do they believe in themselves?

Step seven: Identity

Again, open and close your eyes for the transition into the next square titled Identity. Who are the successful people? What kind of people are they? In your ideal outcome, what identity do they have? Who are they? Are they genuinely successful people that shine and radiate happiness?

Step eight: Life purpose

Quickly blink in order to step into the last square: Life Purpose. What is the mission of the successful people? Who else are they serving other than themselves? What vision do they have? Are they able to be a better mother because they don't have to be stressed out all the time? Are they better to their kids and spouse? Are they able to have a successful career because they have extra time to focus on that because they don't have to spend time worrying about their failure? Are they inspiring others and making their genuine happiness contagious?

MERGE

Step nine: Backward merge

Now take this life purpose and apply it to yourself. Fully merge the life purpose of the successful people with yours. Make it yours. Integrate it as your new purpose. Take a step back and bring this life purpose into the identity square where you will now fully immerse yourself into the identity of the successful people. You are now a successful person. You are now a genuinely successful person that shines and radiates happiness. Step back into each square, into beliefs and values, skills, behaviours and environment and apply the responses that you had envisioned to yourself.

Step ten: Fully embody your desired outcome

Step back completely and enjoy an exhilarating moment fully immersed in your desired outcome.

KEY CONCEPTS:

ACT & MERGE - PROGRAM YOUR BRAIN

In order to fully integrate our desired outcome, we have to act as if we had already achieved it and immerse ourselves in each neurological level to embody each area of ourselves. This process allows us to transform the acting into a fully merged reality.

CHAPTER 39

BE AUTHENTIC

"So, do it. Decide.

Is this the life You want to live?

Is this the person You want to love?

Is this the best you can be?

Can you be stronger?

Kinder? More compassionate?

Decide. Breathe in. Breathe out. And decide."

Meredith Grey, Grey's Anatomy

Are you fixed for good now? You just programmed your brain so that must be the end right? You are good to go forever no? Just like you cannot eat your next twenty-one meals for the whole week today and not have to eat at all this week, you will need to feed your mind again on a daily basis. Fifty percent of people who begin a self-directed program will drop out in the first 6 months. When we are not being monitored, we decrease our chances of success. It is because we lack the mental key.

Is writing your desired, well-formed outcome enough? Can you just store it in a drawer now and completely forget about it? Is doing any of these exercises once, all back to back, enough? You must keep re-doing them until they are part of your way of being. Until they become your daily routine. Until you have a natural habit of amplifying and anchoring positive feelings. Until you can easily act a successful behaviour and make it become yours.

"Success is the sum of small efforts, repeated day in day out." — *Robert Collier*

Keep surrounding yourself with positive people. Just like you need to eat every day, you also need to feed your brain every day. In the next few chapters, you will learn how to prevent negative distracting thoughts from interfering. You will be given tools to cope with special circumstances. You will make a plan B and prepare for uncontrollable factors and learn tricks to maintain your new body.

Now that you are mastering the art of programming your brain, and are fully excited and motivated, you may wonder how to keep this going. How can you feel fully, genuinely authentic?

Nathalie's mom used to tell her that we need to eat food everyday to feed our body but we also need to feed our brain daily. She has developed the habit of downloading audio books that she listens to in the morning as she gets ready for her day. Jack Canfield once said: "You can't put your hand in a bucket of glue, without some of that glue sticking to your hand." So she likes to "audio-read" biographies of successful people, their stories, how they did it and what lessons she can learn from them. She finds that audiobooks work well for her as they can play in the background in the kitchen when she cooks, or in her car while she drives. It is all food for the soul.

Here are some of the author's favourite books:

- A New Earth by Eckhart Tolle
- Awaken the Giant Within by Anthony Robbins
- Change your Brain, Change your Body by Daniel G. Amen
- Gateway to Success and Happiness by Og Mandino
- Get the Life you Want by Richard Bendler
- Good to Great by Jim Collins
- Great by Choice by Jim Collins
- Happy for no Reason by Marci Shimoff
- How to Create the Life you Want by Wayne Dwyer
- How to Overcome your Self Limiting Beliefs & Achieve Anything You Want by Omar Johnson
- Lean In by Sheryl Sandburg
- Le Millionnaire by Marc Fisher
- Mastering Your Mean Girl by Melissa Ambrosini
- Mindset by Carol S. Dweck
- Road to Valor by Aili and Andres McConnon
- Take a Shot by Dave Morrow and Jake Steinfeld
- Success Principles - Jack Canfield
- The 7 Habits of Highly Effective People by Stephen R. Covey
- The 8th Habit by Stephen R. Covey
- The Art of Thinking Clearly by Rolf Dobelli
- The Foundation of Successful Change by Zig Ziglar
- The Life-Changing Magic of Tidying Up by Marie Kondo
- The Motivation Manifesto by Brendon Burchard
- The Purple Cow by Seth Godin

- The Rise of Superman by Steven Kotler
- The Ultimate Gift by Jim Stovall
- The Untethered Soul by Michael A. Singer
- Think and Grow Rich—Napoleon Hill
- Way of the Peaceful Warrior by Dan Millman
- Who Moved My Cheese by Spencer Johnson
- Why People Fail by Simon Reynolds
- Women who Run with the Wolves by Clarissa Pinkola Estes

Start your day off by listening to positive, motivating audiotapes on your iPod or iPhone. If we don't motivate ourselves, then who will? Stay focused. If it's too hard for you to stay motivated, hire a coach. Or join a class with a group of friends who will help you stay on track and stay motivated. Timing is important. If right now for example, you're going through a divorce, you're quitting smoking, changing jobs etc. then right now is probably not the best time for you to start making bold moves towards your journey. Remember to do one thing at a time, take baby steps.

What are you going to do to stay motivated? It's easy after you've just been fed positive information and tools. Your homework now is to put in place the tools you will need to stay motivated. Getting into a good state is mandatory when we are learning and implementing new good habits. If you take problems too seriously, you make them more real. Spending 3 hours a day on Facebook is not a personality trait; it is just a bad habit. Building good feelings should be something you do every day.

What are you going to do to stay motivated?

Example: Exchange phone numbers with people who motivate you. Hire a coach that will hold you accountable for the actions to which you've committed. Do some reading and research. Download audio books. Tell the whole world about how motivated you are about your new life. Choose to spend less time with negative people. Start on this journey with a friend.

Give this book to everyone you know so that you are all on the same page. Use whatever works. Implement some tools to keep you motivated and make them work for you.

1. _____

2. _____

3. _____

We will give you more examples of what you can do in order to stay motivated and on track. The next few chapters are inherent to remaining successful!

KEY CONCEPTS

BE AUTHENTIC

We need to continue to apply all that we have learned already in our daily lives and continue to stay on top of our newly formed habits.

By committing to feeding your brain with positive information on a regular basis, you increase your daily level of motivation.

Choose some techniques you will use to stay motivated.

CHAPTER 40

CHOICES

"Quantum science suggests the existence of many possible futures for each moment of our lives. Each future lies in a state of rest until it is awakened by choices made in the present." — *Gregg Braden*

ARE YOU CHOOSING YOUR LIFE?

Did you know that once the average American reaches sixty years old, they have spent about ten years in front of the television and five years on social media?

Without making any judgment, we can say that it would be totally fine, if it were actually the result of someone's desire to do so. Unfortunately, most people look back on their lives and say: "I wish I had spent more time with my family, or opened up a business, or called my friends more often, or spent more time on my health and went to the gym, but I had no TIME." And yet, they spent 15 years in front of a screen for entertainment!

THE YES AND THE NO PORTIONS OF A CHOICE

Now that you are in charge of your life, you will understand the concept of choice. There are two major aspects to choosing. A choice is a result of a desire, or not. When you choose something, you say YES to it. The other portion of the choice is the NO portion of it. When you say YES to something, by definition, you say NO to everything else. So whenever you decide to do something, you are putting everything else on the back burner.

"People think focus means saying yes to the thing you've got to focus on. But that's not what it means at all. It means saying no to the hundred other good ideas that there are". — *Steve Jobs*

Make sure to set your priorities and that what you choose is really what you want to do. For some people, their friends and families, their biggest dreams, their health, their sleep, etc. are too often what is left behind, while some unimportant matters are chosen to occupy their precious time.

What are you going to say "no" to when you say "yes" to being successful? If you choose to be building a business, you may need to say "no" to putting everybody else first. Spend your leisure time wisely. Time is not wasted if you're doing what you want to do. The key word is intention. If you have important priorities to address and make the conscious decision to sit on a bench and do nothing for an hour to clear your mind, it is fine. If you choose to do nothing and you enjoy it, you are spending your time intentionally. If you spend your time intentionally, then it's not wasted and you will have no regrets. The problems occur when we get caught up wasting time un-intentionally.

Consider Life is a smorgasbord where you get to have it all laid out in front of you. Then CHOOSE that for which you have the greatest appetite. You choose which of those items support your biggest and highest vision of yourself and your life. Life can be so busy and chaotic that we can choose the most accessible thing, just because it is there. Become conscious of your thought process. Become disciplined and aware of the choices you make. Ask yourself, "Does this choice I am about to make bring me closer to my vision? Stall me? Take me further away? It is important to avoid making long-term decisions based on a short-term frame of mind.

"Efficiency is doing the thing right. Effectiveness is doing the right thing."
— *Peter Drucker*

TOWARDS vs AWAY FROM

It is much more appealing to move towards something than away from it. When you are excited about a new project, when your gut is telling you to go for it, that is when you really can drive and move mountains. When you run away from negative things, although it works for some, it is only temporary and sooner than later, you will need something to move towards in order to motivate you. For example, saying YES to a new business that will give you accomplishment, personal satisfaction, leaving legacy for your children, etc. is a lot more convincing than saying NO to being tired, stressed and broke.

"It is our choices, that show what we truly are, far more than our abilities."   — *J.K Rowling*

People make the best choices they can at any given time with the resources that are available to them. The more choices you have, the more you become aware of other options, and the more it empowers you and gives you the tools to change.

KEY CONCEPTS

CHOICE

When you say yes to something, by default, you say no to something else. We tend to be driven more by saying yes to going towards exciting things vs going away from unappealing situations.

Find what you are going towards when you make your choices.

CHAPTER 41

ANTICIPATE

"When one door of happiness closes, another opens; but often we look so long at the closed door that we do not see the one which has been opened for us." — *Helen Keller*

Anticipate. Most likely, the reason why you have been unsuccessful in the past is because you did not know that there were other choices and other alternatives to the behaviours that were causing you to fail.

It is not your personal history that makes you who you are. It is your response to it with the choices that you have available at the time. You can choose what behaviour you want to execute and program them in advance.

We only do the best with what we have. We can never judge anyone. So make sure you avoid judging your past and don't be hard on yourself. In the following exercise, when we go back to an old unwanted behaviour, the only purpose is to identify what triggered this behaviour and replace it with something more useful. We have the mental skills to see what we don't want and to replace it with what we do want. Change is the only constant in life. Everything in life is temporary. Be in charge of the change that will happen to you, the direction you will go, and what you will become. Don't wait for life to happen to you.

"The best way to predict the future is to create it."

Peter F. Drucker

A friend of Nathalie recently purchased one of those wrist devices that calculate your number of daily steps. It even comes with an app on her phone where she can enter the food that she eats, and it will help her identify how many calories she has consumed and spent during the day. The calories-in-calories-out technique is something that has worked for her. Nathalie personally has one of these watches and she is using it mainly to track her sleep. Nathalie's friend did not know that this watch could do that. She taught her how to find that information inthe app and they started comparing our sleep patterns. Nathalie said that she had slept 8 hours and 16 minutes and then it described her sleep quality. She had been awake one time during 8 hours, she had been restless 6 times and she had spent 9 minutes alternating between awake and restless. Her friends numbers were really different. She had slept for 9 hours 23 minutes. She had been awake 59 times, restless for 4 hours and had spent 3 hours alternating between awake and restless. She was stunned. Now if you are wondering where we are going with this story, here it comes. Her friend said: "I did not know it was possible to sleep through the night like you do. I knew that my sleep was bad, but I did not know the extent of it. I thought that it was normal to turn around and take hours before falling asleep and wake up many times during the night."

This was a huge revelation to her. She did not know. When the resource became available to her, she tracked her sleep and watched her numbers go down. She kept telling Nathalie what a big light bulb moment that had been for her. Now she could start having a good night's sleep because she now knew it was possible. She had increased her choices and she was starting to program her brain to sleep profoundly. Now she believed it could be done.

It is time to foresee what can stand between you and your desired outcome. In this chapter, you will develop a Plan B. Let's say you had intended to go to a networking meeting this week, but something got in the way of your intention. Anticipate what could happen and have a plan for it.

First, you will identify the threats. Only you can know what has created your past un-successes. After listing what you think could happen, you will prepare some responses that will keep you on track with your new life.

HERE ARE SOME EXAMPLES:

You have experienced in the past that the week goes by without you having had time to work on your marketing. If you see that this could happen again in the future, you will now have a marketing schedule ready, prepared in advance with some options and you will commit to it. Don't wait until you're tired to do your planning. We don't think or plan well when we're tired.

If you noticed that you were being "weak" (making poor choices) while choosing who to hang out with at a function, you will now always make a list that supports your networking plan and you will stick to it. You will plan in advance and even send emails to those you absolutely want to connect with at a certain event.

If your downfall has been the fact that you tend to go off track a lot, you will now know to time yourself when doing a task and stay on track, until that task is done.

Have a "What If" plan. What if you get called into a meeting at lunch time when you were planning to work on your personal business?

You will have a time planned in the afternoon to catch up on your personal agenda.

What if everyone is going out for brunch on Saturday morning when you had planned to work on your accounting? You will take an hour to work on your books and then meet them later, as people always arrive late anyway. By the time they order, you will get there just in time for the food... or better even, eat at home quickly before you go. What you want really is to hang out with your friends, not the food.

Always take control and have a backup plan. Set yourself up for success. Don't let yourself be surprised. Know in advance. I know you already have a lot of ideas in your head! You know what distractions are presented to you! No more surprises! Be in charge now. Take control and do a conscious vision and plan for when you don't feel you're 100%. And always give the 100% you have. Prepare, prepare, prepare. Always have a Plan B. Always prepare for things you can't control.

> *"Obstacles are those frightful things you see when you take your eyes off your goal."* — Henry Ford

Here you go. List some obstructions that could get in the way of your success.

Obstructions
Anticipate the things that could get in the way

1. _____

2. _____

3. _____

4. _____

5. _____

Find an alternative for them – what's your Plan B?

1. _____

2. _____

3. _____

4. _____

5. _____

This tool will help you plan for new better serving behaviours. Now we know we can plan ahead for behaviours. But can we also plan for our feelings? Can we plan to be in the mood for working? Can we fake it until we make it? In her study about physiological behaviour and psychological responses, social psychologist Amy Cuddy comes to the conclusion that in fact, we can not only fake it until we make it, but we can fake it until we become it.

This is what you will learn about in the next chapter.

KEY CONCEPTS

ANTICIPATE

You more than likely know some scenarios that could get in the way of your new lifestyle.

By anticipating these situations, you can plan ahead what you will choose to do, instead of your old negative behaviour.

CHAPTER 42

MIND & BODY CONNECTION

"A good stance and posture reflect a proper state of mind."
— *Morihei Ueshiba*

The mind and the body are connected. Each affects the other. Let's say for example, when you are tired, you curl up in a chair. Your brain associates the state of mind with the physical behaviour and then reverses the two: conversely, slumping in your chair can make you feel tired. The cause is now the effect and the effect is now the cause. Wouldn't it be great if we could just think about a state of mind that we want to feel, and consciously enter it?

It is very much possible and, at one point of your life, you have already proven that fact. You know when you are having a bad day but it happens to be your 3 years old daughter's birthday? You can immediately "force" yourself to enter a happy mood in order to make the occasion great for her. Or when you feel down and you have to meet with your boss' boss? You fake it and then before you know it, you are entering a different mood.

Amy Cuddy, social psychologist, demonstrated how our body language shapes who we are.

Body language is communication and interaction. It decides whom we ask out on a date, whom we choose to hire or promote. We are influenced by non-verbal communication, i.e. our feelings, our thoughts, our physiology, our non-verbal expressions of power and dominance. For example in the animal kingdom, we have all seen pictures of how animals expand, stretch themselves out and open up to show pride and power. The reverse is also true. When powerless, we make ourselves small.

In life, when interacting with others, we complement the other person's behaviour. If they are making themselves powerful, we tend to do the opposite.

Amy Cuddy responded to the question: "Can you fake it till you make it?" Can we choose to experience a behavioural outcome that makes us feel more powerful? We know that our non-verbal behaviours govern how other people think and feel about us. But the real question, in her research was: "Do our non-verbal actions govern how we think and feel about ourselves?"

Our mind changes our bodies and our bodies change our mind. In Cuddy's study, where the subjects needed to take a high power pose (standing with their chest up) or low power pose (sitting and curled up), their levels of cortisol (stress hormone) and testosterone (dominant hormone) changed significantly. The subjects in high power poses became more assertive, confident and comfortable. The subjects in the low power poses became very stress-reactive and had feelings of 'shutting down'.

Our nonverbal body language governs how we think and feel about ourselves. So yes, our bodies change our minds. Can power posing for a few minutes really change your life in meaningful ways? In Cuddy's study, high power posers had more presence. They were more passionate, enthusiastic, confident, captivating, comfortable and authentic. So our bodies change our minds, our minds change our behaviour and our behaviour changes our outcomes. Even when we say 'fake it until you make it', we don't really want to get the result and feel like a fraud or an imposter. So we don't only 'fake it 'til we make it' but 'fake it 'til we become it'! Tiny tweaks can lead to big changes.

Knowing that your physiology is really impacting who you are, use this knowledge to your advantage. Just ask yourself at any given time: "How would I like to feel right now, what mood would I like to be in?" And proceed to enter the mood you want. Next time you are sitting at work and are about to start a task that you are unfamiliar with, don't curl up, bring your hands behind your head, spread out, and be in a powerful pose so you will more likely be able to attack that task ahead.

Look confident. Put your body in a confident position. Give yourself this opportunity. Give yourself 5 seconds. Have you already made changes in the way you were standing or sitting as you are reading these words? Curling up might feel comfortable but if you are ready and know what you want, start looking like it. Change your position and look confident. Head up, chest lifted. You will get better results. You are in the process of gaining control over your body.

POWER POSING

Mo always use the scenario of standing in front of your full length mirror first thing in the morning and saying "It's going to be a great day." It is hard to belief yourself if you are slouched over (with poor posture) and looking tired. Instead, if you stand strong (and power up your posture) it is easier to convince your mind that it's going to be a great day when you stand tall and look proud. It is also important to choose your words wisely. If you look outside and it's raining or snowing, and you are looking tired (standing hunched over) and you say "It is going to be a crappy day", your mind will interpret it exactly that way. If instead you actualize your state with positive words along with a power pose, your words will influence your thoughts, your thoughts will influence your actions and you will immediately influence your physical state (look, feel, believe).

When Mo teaches power posing and attaches a verbal mantra using I am... I can... I will... that is when she gets the best results.

> *Example: "I am great!" "I can smile more today!" "I will stand on stage with pride!" "I am strong!" "I can fake it until I make it!" "I will make it a great day!".*

Complementing the physiology with spoken driving words will also complement the technique. Mo also believes that what you think about expands. So when you power pose and you think about yourself being strong and invincible and you say it out loud, you soon magnifiy that thought further. It then expands until you can feel it vibrate in your whole body. While this vibrational energy is subtle, it is powerful.

Mo has a great story about preparing yourself mentally: "Twenty years ago, I was in Australia presenting at a conference. I had injured myself the night before, and I hadn't slept very much because I was in pain. I was supposed to teach a 5-hour workshop starting very early in the morning. I distinctly remember nurturing my body with 1.5 liters of water. I couldn't eat because I didn't feel well. Before my presentation, I went to the ladies bathroom and I stood in front of the mirror and I said out loud, "I am confident and

I will be the most inspirational, motivating, and knowledgeable leader on this topic; I will go out there and I will make an impact!" I looked in the mirror, said it out loud, with affirmation, confidence, and boldness. And as I walked out of the bathroom, I noticed that there were two women in the stalls who were probably fearful

of walking out, thinking that I thought I was alone, and they didn't want to embarrass me for having talked out loud. The best part of all was there was no other workshop that morning,

so those two women came to my session! I'll never forget that. I wanted to make a great impression and I did. It was the best presentation, or one of the best, I've ever given in my career."

3 POSES

Here are three poses you will enjoy. To get the most of these poses, practice in front of a mirror. Eventually, you will be able to feel it as you do it. As you pose, verbalize the mantra out loud and internalize it.

1. "Superwoman Pose" (standing with fists on hips, chest lifted, shoulders back, core braced... no cape required)
2. "Strong Pose" (arms lifted shoulder level with elbows bent at 90 degrees, flexing to show off your biceps... no pipes required)
3. "Victory Pose" (arms lifted overhead and wide like the letter "V"... no finish line required)

Enjoy power posing and, remember; striking a pose is not only powerful for your mind, it makes you feel stronger and sexier! Caution: These poses might lead to a smile or an uncontrollable grin.

> ### KEY CONCEPTS
> #### MIND & BODY CONNECTION
> Mind and body are connected. You can use your physiology in order to change your state of mind.
>
> Power posing with a verbal mantra is a great tool to instantly change your mindset into the positive.

CHAPTER 43

15 MINUTE MORNING SUCCESS ROUTINE

"Some people dream of success while other people wake up every morning and make it happen." — *Wayne Huizenga*

This 15-minute morning SUCCESS routine will become your ritual: SUCCESS is an acronym for a 7-step method.

Sit in Silence

Understand

Construct

Create

Energize

Scribe

Stretch

This SUCCESS ritual is a simple process however it requires work— the discipline to take consistent daily action, first thing upon rising. To achieve the success you desire you must be willing to match your level of desire with the same level of action and commitment to daily self-mastery. Self-mastery requires self-discipline around how you think, feel and act. Challenge yourself to this ritual first thing every morning for 30 days in a row and own your day!

"S"

Sit in Silence/Silence- and/or meditate (to become mindful of your breathing, your thoughts, feelings). —5 minutes

"U"

Understand and identify one strength that you will bring to your success today. Choose and complete one of these three statements to help clarify a strength today. —1 minute

I am…._____, today.

I can… _____, today

I will…. _____, today.

    Example: "I am passionate about my work I need to complete, today."

"C"

Construct a picture in your mind of the future and how things will be, look and feel when you reach your goal —1 minute

"C"

Create one mantra (a positive statement also known as an affirmation) you will verbalize aloud 5 times to confirm your belief in achieving your goal. Choose and complete one of these three affirming statement. —1 minute

I am _____, today.

I can … _____, today

I will…_____, today.

    Example: "I am proud to be a successful and dynamic business woman, today!"

"E"

Energize your mind with personal reading and reflection on new ideas. —5 minutes

"S"

Scribe in a journal what you are most excited about, proud of having achieved or grateful for on this day. —1 minute

"S"

Stretch and move to energize your body (to increase your heart rate and respiratory rate), or practice your high power-poses learned in the previous chapter to build confidence and set your state for the day.—1 minute

KEY CONCEPTS

Starting the day with this fifteen minutes SUCCESS routine will set the tone for the remainder of the day. Fifteen minutes is really short compared to all the time you will save by starting the day on the right foot.

CHAPTER 44

AMPLIFY POSITIVE FEELINGS

"The difference between the ordinary and the extraordinary is that little EXTRA." — *Jimmy Johnson*

People are drawn to your energy, to what you are and what you stand for. Not your skills or intelligence or material possessions. They are drawn to the state you are in. The good news is that you can make yourself feel great by sending yourself nice messages on a regular basis. It is all about mental rehearsing. Remember things that make you feel good all the time. Expect to feel good all the time. Shift your belief that feeling good is only for special days. When you feel great, it is easy to exercise and to choose healthy food. Believe that life is meant to make you feel good all the time. Believe it so deeply that, unconsciously, your mind will do what is necessary to feel good.

This technique is designed to allow you to feel great and be your best whenever you want. Usually, the road to success starts well; you are motivated and you are doing everything right. You are on a mission and you are getting results. You love it and it is even kind of easy. Then, somehow, it starts to plateau and you find your motivation lowering and somehow, all the great feelings you had are going down the drain and everything seems so much harder. How great will that be when you are able to amplify your positive feelings so you can make them last? This is exactly what you will learn with this exercise.

STEP ONE: IDENTIFY A POSITIVE FEELING TO AMPLIFY

Close your eyes and think about one of the best feelings you have ever had in regards to your success. You felt amazing. Maybe you were on a roll. Maybe you were feeling powerful. You had your Mojo going. See what you saw and hear what you heard when you felt that good feeling. As you do so, notice where this really amazing feeling comes from. Where in your body does it start? Where does it move? When you stop thinking about the feeling, where does it go? Notice the pattern of the feeling. Pull it back up and embrace it fully, then stop thinking about it and notice how it ends.

STEP TWO: AMPLIFICATION

Go back to that amazing feeling, and let it come up fully. Grasp it generously and just before it goes away, imagine pulling it out of your body and place it back where it begins, so that it moves in a circle. Spin it round and round and faster and faster. Notice that, as you spin it faster, the feeling gets stronger. Experience how much pleasure your body is truly capable of. Feel the exhilaration of this amazing state.

By doing so, you are reinforcing the neural pathway that was created when experiencing this for the first time and you are amplifying the feeling and putting it at the top of the pile so that it is readily available for you whenever you feel that your motivation starts to deflate.

Being in a state of confidence helps in trusting your abilities to succeed. This time, whenever there are obstacles in your success journey, you will be able to go right back into that resourceful state and find strength and energy to do whatever you need to do to make this work. With amplified positive feelings, you don't have to know everything because it allows you to believe in your ability to learn and to adapt so you can continue to progress. Learn what needs to be learned and do what needs to be done. Will there be challenges? Maybe. You can power through anything. I know you already have a degree of excellence. You are here reading these pages aren't you? You have already committed. Now use this confidence to get to the next step and take action.

Repeat this exercise every day, and every time something great happens. Live it fully and amplify it. So that eventually, at the top of your pile, there will only be great amazing states ready to be experienced and re-loaded again to the surface.

KEY CONCEPTS

AMPLIFY POSITIVE FEELINGS

You can mentally rehearse positive feelings and amplify them in order to have them accessible to you at any given time.

CHAPTER 45

ANCHORING

"Courage is like a muscle. We strengthen it by use." ~ *Ruth Gordo*

Anchoring. We just mentioned in Amplify Positive Feelings that the state you are in influences your results. Now we will learn how to actually recall one of these amplified feelings. It's just like pushing a "feel-good-button."

Here is an exercise to trigger a positive feeling with the skill of anchoring. You can use it whenever you are about to make a choice related to your success journey and, frankly, in any type of situation. We learned in previous chapters that the mind and body are connected. An emotional feeling can trigger a physical response and the reverse can also happen. A physical stimulus can trigger an emotional state.

"Quality is not an act, it is a habit." — *Aristotle*

Step one: Recall the positive feeling to be anchored

Imagine a movie screen in front of you with a button control connected to what you see on the screen. Go back in your mind to a time, a specific time, when you had a really great experience. Feel the feelings that you felt back then. Perhaps you will imagine a scene when you were working on a fun project. Or a memory of a time you were successful at organizing your day or a time you know that you had lots of willpower. Feel free to use one of your previously amplified positive feelings.

Step one: Amplify the positive feeling to be anchored

Picture the image getting bigger and closer. Live it as the feeling increases. Be "associated", that is, be the main character, seeing the experience through your own eyes (as opposed to be a third person looking at yourself

- dissociated). As this happens, imagine that the button control says 'awesome' and slowly imagine turning it up. To make it feel even more real, as the feeling intensifies, make the physical gesture with the button with your hand. As you turn it up, at the rate that fits the changes, allow that exhilarating memory to get closer, bigger and brighter. Add colour to it, make it shine, look at all the details. Hear a voice in your head that says: "I am awesome! This is amazing!"

Step two: Anchor

At this moment, when you are fully imprinted with the feeling, apply pressure to a part of your body, which will become the kinesthetic anchor for this awesome state of mind. You can choose the anchor to be a specific spot on your hand, on your knuckle, on the back of your neck, etc. Choose a specific spot that you can recall easily. Please avoid common anchors like pressing your hands together, which you do usually in other states (i.e. when you are nervous or when you are cold) because that could send wrong messages to your brain without you noticing. So choose something specific that will only be used to recall positive feelings.

Step three: Neutral

Enjoy this sensation for an instant or two, then release the anchor and let your body come back to a more neutral state.

Step four: Repeat

Repeat the process a few times. It is important to apply the anchor at the peak of the emotional state. It is really important that you do repeat the process at least three times in order to avoid sending mixed messages to your brain. So before going to step five, you must make sure that your brain knows exactly what to do when you press the anchor.

Step five: Test

To verify that the anchoring was successful, remember a moment when you were not at your best. Go there now and feel how it felt. In this negative state, the application of pressure on the anchor will reverse your state and make you feel great instead. Press the anchor as you say to yourself: "I am awesome!" You will find yourself going to a feeling as ecstatic as before.

You can chose anywhere on your body. Nathalie uses a physical anchor on herself. She has a spot right behind her neck that she presses firmly with three fingers every time she is in a great mood. When she finishes a conference or a seminar that went really well, when she witnesses a client succeeding in something, at the end of a great fitness class where she was at her best, when something great happens to her or simply, when she feels like a million bucks! She has been anchoring these feelings right behind her neck for years. And now, whenever she needs a boost, whenever some external pressure comes to her, she just presses the back of her neck with her three fingers and her brain thinks that it needs to generate these exhilarating feelings, which works every time. She immediately gets a rush of great warm sensations, which helps her go through whatever is presenting itself to her at the time.

Remember to keep adding on to your anchor, anytime you experience a great feeling. First, amplify it and then anchor it. Keep stacking more and more so that you make your anchor solid and powerful.

SPACIAL ANCHORING

We have just learned physical anchoring. You can also use a space anchor. Here is the process that we call the Circle of Excellence.

Step one: Set up the space

Imagine a circle big enough so that you could easily step into it. Give it a colour and visualize it. Place it on the floor in front of you and stand just behind it.

Step two: Recall the positive feeling to be anchored

Think of a specific time when you were at your best or when you were easily able to perform the behaviour that you are trying to achieve. For

example, if you are feeling lazy and don't feel like going to work, think of a time where you were going to work regularly and effortlessly. Get into that specific feeling, the same way as above, being associated in the memory, seeing it through your own eyes and increasing the awesomeness of the event.

Step three: Anchor

When you are at the peak of the moment, step into the circle of excellence. Hold the feeling there for a moment until you feel that it starts fading away. When it does, leave the feeling in the circle as you step out.

Step four: Test

Test the circle of excellence. Get into a neutral feeling. Step into the circle of excellence. Notice if your mood changes and adopt the feelings that were left for you in your circle.

You can use the same circle for lots of situations or have different coloured circles that would match various desired states.

KEY CONCEPTS

ANCHORING

You can store positive feelings in a physical or spatial anchor and recall them when you need them simply by triggering the anchor.

The anchor can be a physical point on your body or the action of stepping into an imaginary circle on the floor.

CHAPTER 46

WOMEN WHO INFLUENCE

"I never dreamed about success. I worked for it." — Estee Lauder

We have given you internal success techniques. Here is now an external way of getting support in your road towards achieving your dreams.

Canadian women are playing an increasingly important role in the fabric of the workplace because they now make up almost fifty percent of the workforce. If you want to be successful in your given field, get to know the people who are already successful in it. Surround yourself with like-minded women you look up to, and soak in everything they say and do. Better yet, when the opportunity presents, invite them to join you for a coffee or tea, ask questions and learn from them. Building a relationship with a variety of people who inspire you is key to unlocking your own success. There is a reason you look up to these people, they are positive role models, they are mentors and they are influencers. They have reached impressive heights in their careers and have a story to tell and a willingness to share.

Working hand-in-hand with canfitpro (the Canadian Fitness Professionals), Mo launched the "Women Who Influence" event in 2014 at the 'world fitness expo', Canada's largest fitness education conference and expo. Women Who Influence began as a half-day celebration and networking event for accomplished women in the fitness industry. With each year, more women flock to this event (from all industries) for the engaging conversations and networking and for inspirational lessons gained through the women sharing their journeys and lessons learned along the way. Being surrounded by smart, strong and fit women who have built successful careers is inspiring. If you have attended such an event you will agree. Women are for the most part great networkers, nurturers and teachers but are often under-recognized or appreciated. Events such as Women Who Influence give women the opportunity to be celebrated, validated, appreciated and accepted. Women who influence others with their own unique strengths are at an advantage to forge strong relationships and ignite win-win opportunities. The power of women working and learning together is unlimited. These are ten of the many lessons shared from some of the best Women Who Influence events:

1. Be bold, dream big, define your greatness and own it. Write your story and own it. This is your life so live it out loud.

2. Say YES! Embrace both opportunity and challenge and welcome the opportunity to learn and grow every day.

3. Have the courage to challenge the status quo. While easier said than done, strive to continually learn to embrace change because you will be stronger and better for it and have a greater sense of pride and purpose.

4. Have the confidence to be positively disruptive, to be remembered. Challenge mediocrity in both yourself and others. Trust your talents, instinct or 'super power'.

5. Possess the willingness to work hard, stay focused and take disciplined action until you succeed. These are leader-ship-style strengths and principles to guide you.

6. Believe in you! Decide and define your role (how you will success and serve the world), what your life will be, and what role you will play.

7. Do not play small. You are not here, in this life, to play small. Do not let anyone or anything tell you otherwise.

8. Share your story and let you light shine.

9. Allow your passion to provide you with the fuel to drive your purpose forward.

10. Embrace fears as an important part of your journey. Lean in and embrace failure as a life lesson and your flaws as beauty spots.

"To accomplish great things we must not only act, but also dream, not only plan, but also believe." — *Anatole France*

KEY CONCEPTS

Be brave and reach out to the leaders in the industry in which you are striving to succeed. The lessons learned from powerful women and valuable insights you gain can be applied in your own life. Surround yourself with people who inspire you.

CHAPTER 47

BUILD YOUR OWN CIRCLE OF INFLUENCE

"Watch for the people whose eyes light up when you talk about your dream. Those are the people you keep." — *Elizabeth Gilbert*

One of the best ways to ensure that your own success is inevitable is to surround yourself with a like-minded community. Women in business, who support each other with powerful intentions, create a strong force for change and success. You can use this book as a means to create and grow a like-minded community. Then you will have a source of support, inspiration, accountability, and a safe container in which to share and grow the most powerful version of yourself.

There are a number of ways in which you can do this:

1) The simplest way is to **create a book club (**or a book and wine club if you prefer!)

As you begin to THINK Yourself™ SUCCESSFUL, your brain will be retrained to look for new opportunities that align with your highest purpose. Reading this book and actively engaging with the workbook alone is a good start. Creating a community, even if you begin as only two people, will bolster your confidence, trigger creativity, and engage your brain with a clear intention for moving forward. Helping others also triggers a strong chemical response in the brain, and makes us feel good, which will further enhance your own experience.

2) **Create a workout group** that integrates journaling work from the book.

Nathalie, Mo and Tasha will all tell you that the path to success is accelerated when you engage the brain and body in concert.

3) As a group, **attend a training** with any or all of the authors. Shared excitement over a common inspirational experience is a great way to keep momentum going!

OUR SUPER POWER

We are all different and when we get together with other powerful women, we soon realize we are all bringing something to the table. We each have a super power. Your power associates with your identity. It is what allows you to live fully your life purpose. Depending on who you are, it can be your gut instinct, your heart or your head. One of them shows you the way. This is your super power. It is what you refer to naturally when facing anything in order to get the answers you need.

What is your Super Power?

Example:

Mo's super power is to trust her '2nd voice', which is her gut instinct and to use the strength she has been given to speak up and share her vision, her thoughts and feelings, no matter if they are incongruent with everyone else. Mo knows that when she doesn't listen to her 2nd voice, she regrets it. Many times, she has learned that her 2nd voice was, in fact, right.

Nathalie's superpower is to take a big picture idea and break it down into steps, create logical processes and easy to follow systems, explaining in layman's terms what needs to be done so that everybody can be on the same page and understand the tasks they need to do to reach a common goal.

Tasha's superpower is the ability to 'see' the best in others, the vulnerabilities and the strengths, and to hold the highest vision of them until they can hold/own it for themselves. This is her greatest calling in Life. When she embraces that, she is energized and Life also flows for her.

What is yours?

_____

_____

_____

_____

When you participate or organize any type of event, make sure you are prepared with what you want them to remember from you, who you are and what is your super power.

HOW DO YOU INTRODUCE YOURSELF?

When asked: "What do you do?" Do you find yourself lost for words, or overwhelming your audience with too much information? Scripting a short thirty-second introduction and learning it so that it naturally flows will create confidence when you are asked this question again. We like to call it the Elevator Pitch. If you were in an elevator and only had a few seconds before the person would exit to their floor, what would you say?

CREATE YOUR ELEVATOR PITCH

The first part of the elevator pitch is a simple sentence that states what you do as you shake their hand.

Hi, I am ... and I ...

> *Example: "Hi, I'm Nathalie. I write books, I am a Coach and a Speaker."*

Then you have to be prepared to add on more meat, in case they ask you for more (and they will). This second part needs to portrait a problem that you solve so that they or someone they know can relate to.

> *Example: "Do you know someone who was all motivated for a while and then somehow they lost their mojo? They know what they can do but they can't seem to find it inside themselves anymore. Well, I have designed a system for people to program themselves to discover their full potential "*

The last part of the elevator pitch would be in a situation where you are at a function and would meet someone who doesn't have enough information after the first two sentences. They want to know more. Here is an example of what you would say.

> *Example: "My brand is called THINK Yourself™. (THINK Yourself™ SUCCESSFUL, THIN Yourself™ THIN, THINK Yourself™ WEALTHY, etc.) It is a three steps system that combines all six layers of your brain to work together and guide you to living a fulfilling life.*

SHIFT THE FOCUS ONTO OTHERS

Even if you are prepared with your script, it doesn't mean that people want to hear it. Wait until you are asked. You may spend a full evening with someone and never really divulge anything about yourself. Be more interested than interesting. Be the one asking the question "What do you do?" Use sentences like: "Tell me more..." People love talking about themselves. Once the focus has been on them for a while, they may say: "Okay, enough about me, what do YOU do?" And then, you will have their complete attention. They may not even ask. They will remember you even if you haven't said a word. If you make them talk, they will come home and say to their significant other: "Wow, I just met this amazing lady, she is absolutely awesome, we had such a great evening!" The reason why they will have felt that way will be because you will have made them talk about themselves first.

Making people feel good about themselves and feel important and listened to is a powerful rapport-building skill. Remember, you have two ears and one mouth for a reason.

KEY CONCEPTS

BUILD YOUR OWN CIRCLE OF INFLUENCE

Surrounding yourself with other like-minded women will keep you focused.

YOUR SUPER POWER

Understanding how everybody brings something different to the table, and knowing our personal super power, allows you to fully live your life purpose.

KNOW HOW TO INTRODUCE YOURSELF

Scripting and rehearsing your elevator pitch with allow you to introduce yourself with confidence.

SHIFT THE FOCUS ON THEM

Make sure you ask the other person to tell them about themselves first.

CHAPTER 48

BE ACCOUNTABLE

"Accountability is the glue that ties commitment to results".
— *Bob Proctor.*

Accountable. This chapter will help you commit to some actions. You can't reach your new lifestyle if you think that *someday* you will start enjoying your work and *someday* you will start being successful. *Someday* is a code for "never." Your someday has yet to come and will forever be this unnamed day. Turn someday into TODAY. You can be as successful as you want to be. Now.

In order to be accountable to yourself, make a list of concrete actions or behaviours that you will commit to doing. Choose your actions according to the areas that you identified at the beginning of the book. Remember when you filled out your wheel?

List three things that you are going to do this week if you want to bring your pie slices up closer to 10. We are not aiming for a 10 necessarily. Just aim for one more point. If you have given yourself a 4, what can cause this 4 to increase to a 5?

Choose 1 slice of your wheel first. Write one to three things that you can do this week in order to increase the number by 1.

I choose to work on the slice called: _____

List 3 things you will do this Week to make this slice of the pie go up of one point: **short term action**

  1. _____

  2. _____

  3. _____

Remember that these commitments can be anchored, amplified, etc. with all the techniques you have learned. Take these actions and actualize them with the tools that have worked for you so far.

Once the actions you committed to above are easy and on-going new habits, you will work on the following three new things: **long term actions**

1. _____

2. _____

3. _____

There is power in setting up the intentions and installing them into your unconscious mind. Now that you know how this works, you will constantly be amazed at how much your life has shifted and changed in light of all this new knowledge.

KEY CONCEPTS

ACCOUNTABLE

By writing down the specific and concrete actions you want to commit to, you are making yourself accountable.

You want to use all the tools you have learned so far to process these new commitments in your brain.

CHAPTER 49

BE APPRECIATIVE

"She is clothed with strength and dignity and laughs without fear of the future." — *unknown*

Appreciate. Take the time to enjoy life and your successes. Use the D.N.A System for everything you would like to change in your life. 'Success' is only one area where this amazing system has been successful.

Now you know the system. First, you start with setting up your DESIRE and use the tools that I have provided you to decide on a compelling outcome. Then, you clean up your past in order to create a NEW YOU, free of negative emotions and limiting beliefs. And lastly, you ACTUALIZE your desire with the programming techniques that you have learned and make sure your NEW YOU is permanent.

As you create your new life, take some time to slow down and appreciate little things. Train yourself to feel good, like you train your muscles. Feeling good is a physiological response, so you CAN train it. Be excited and enthusiastic! Whatever life brings you, you are now in control of how you respond to it. Choose to respond in a dynamic and fun way. You are making it up anyways! You might as well create your new life expecting it to be absolutely amazing!

Nathalie likes to make a "have-done-list". It makes her feel happy now. We all know very well how the "to-do-list" makes us feel. Make a list of what you have done instead. It is very empowering. We all have done great things that made us grow in the past. Use it to make you feel great. You are awesome. Why wait for something great to happen in order for us to feel amazing? Feel great now! Have you ever heard yourself say: "I will be happy when this week is over?" Why wait for the week to be over to be happy. Just be happy now.

Remember that you have the ability to manage your state. Make sure you choose your life and who you surround yourself with.

Create a world where it is easy to dream what you want to be, write down what you want and do what you wrote. And remember to always do one thing at a time, consistently.

Don't just Be. Be Your Best.

> *"I can't think of anything more beautiful than someone who is unafraid to be herself."*   — *Emma Stone*

KEY CONCEPTS

BE APPRECIATIVE
Enjoy your life. You only live once.

CHAPTER 50

ABOUT THE AUTHORS
MAUREEN HAGAN

Influencing positive change for women worldwide @mo_hagan, www.mohagan.com

Mo is a global Health and Wellness Expert, No. 1 Best-selling Author, Speaker, International Award-Winning Program Director and Fitness Instructor. Mo is a licensed Physiotherapist and certified Fitness Instructor and has been recognized for her work in fitness that has spanned over three decades; named as one of *Canada's 20 Most Influential Woman in Sport and Physical Activity*, the International Fitness Industry's *Woman of the Year* and a *Top 100 Health Influencer in Canada*.

You're Off to Great Places!

Today is your day!

Your mountain is waiting.

So get on your way!

Dr Seuss, Oh, the Places You'll Go!

Mo dreamed up her career in fitness having written in her high school graduation year book *"Anything to do with fitness where I can travel the world, teach and lead people to live fit and healthy lives"*. Academically Mo was not the smartest student. Athletically Mo was not strong or fast enough. While

Mo lacked the skills and self-confidence at times, she leveraged her natural ability to withstand rejection, think herself positive and pursue her dreams and the posture to stand up against rejection and negative influencers. Instead, Mo powered up her natural high energy 'never-quit' attitude and practiced harder and longer than most of her school friends and teammates on sport teams in high-school and university and overtime cultivated a level of confidence and self-belief, not to mention disciplined learning habits and resilience.   Without business schooling or experience she climbed the corporate ladder at GoodLife Fitness, Canada's largest fitness chain, where today she holds a position of Vice President of Program Innovation and Fitness Development at both GoodLife Fitness and canfitpro (Canadian Fitness Professionals), a company that she helped to start in 1993.   She has risen to the top of her industry globally, a profession that she was told did not exist but that obviously did not stop her. Mo curated a career in health and fitness, re-shaping health care along the way. With numerous awards for her passion, innovation, instruction and leadership she is most proud of being inducted into her high school in 2009 for her career success.

"To live your greatest life requires a relentless belief in your inner fire. Your Vision becomes a compass and a lighthouse during the darker times when those around you attempt to douse your flame".   — *Gerry Visca*

It is Mo's life mission to help improve the lives of people and she lives to serve the world by inspiring others and helping them succeed by connecting them with people, programs, resources and services that will assist them in finding their own personal health and wellness. While working fulltime as an executive leader at both GoodLife Fitness and canfitpro Mo continues to teach group fitness classes, create group fitness programs that attract exercisers of all ages, she speaks at health and fitness, and business conferences around the world and is a regular contributor to consumer magazines and on-line publications including the Huffington Post. She is a No. 1 best-selling author and recognized fitness authority in Canada. Like any great artist, Mo learned to sculpt her boldness and cultivate her inner confidence and find her own voice. She is living the dream life she envisioned creating and she is an influencer of change, helping to inspire new levels of awareness for fitness, health and wellbeing worldwide. She believes that we are all there to serve the world in our own special way. By honoring our own unique gifts, we inspire others around us to be and do the same.

TASHA HUGHES

"Living a Gorgeous Life @ Tasha Hughes", www.tashahughes.com

"Go and love someone exactly as they are. And then watch how quickly they transform into the greatest and truest version of themselves. When one feels seen and appreciated in their own essence, one is instantly empowered." — *Wes Angelozzi*

Born into a long line of strong-willed Hungarian women, Tasha was taught that LOVE is the most powerful force in the universe, and FAITH in herself as a contributing part of something much bigger, is the foundation for living a happy life.

Tasha Hughes is a Women's Empowerment Coach, No.1 Best-selling Author, Speaker, Seminar Facilitator, Black Belt in Karate, Yoga Teacher and Therapist, with 25 years in the fields of Health and Wellness. Creator of the Neuroscience of Thriving Strategies and Innovator of Diva Defence: Age-Defying Wellness and Self-Protection Fitness; her programs integrate neuroscientific research with complimentary modalities, to deliver excellent brain/body strategies for the 2nd half of life.

Her broad educational background reflects her curious nature. She studied Journalism at Carleton University, Spanish at Universidad de Autonoma in Madrid, World Religions, as well as an Independent Research Study on the Neurophysiology of Meditation, at the

University of Waterloo. She was accepted into the Neuroscience Program at Dalhousie University (but chose love and a family instead). Her passion for Neuroscience continues, and is vital to her most recent offerings.

As the "crowning jewel" of her combined education and experience, Tasha created the 6-level curriculum, "Diva Defence", a hybrid of yoga, martial arts, and self-empowerment for women over 40. Diva Defence is the cognitive fitness correlate of the other leg of her coaching practice: The Neuroscience of Thriving Educational Seminars. At the time of writing this book, Tasha was preparing an online offshoot of Diva called, "Sexy, Playful and Strong: Redefining Yourself After Life Falls Apart." You can find Tasha through her new Facebook page, "Living a Gorgeous Life @ Tasha Hughes", or her website: www.tashahughes.com

Until the breakdown of her marriage, Tasha had been lucky and successful at everything she set her mind to. The end of that relationship marked the end of a "charmed life" in many ways, as she had to face the shame and sense of failure that it created. It was then that all of her beliefs, skills and knowledge were tested. It was THE true test of all she claimed to live by. It was also that event that ultimately set her on her present course, to work with women based on her own life experience, and create environments in which women can redefine themselves after their perceived 'failures' in life.

"Above all, be the heroine of your own life, not the victim." – Nora Ephron

Tasha comes by her desire to thrive honestly. Born in "smalltown South Western Ontario", to a Mother who modeled for her what it means to set your intentions high, create a strong vision for yourself, and then set about the details to make it happen. Despite the difficulties and hardships that resulted from her own divorce, Tasha's Mom worked full-time, dedicating 10 years of her life commuting to night school in order to finish her university education, and went on to have a highly successful career in corporate PR. Tasha grew up watching her Mom as a local TV celebrity. With a strong philanthropic streak, she volunteered for many local charity boards. In her retirement, she has turned to her passion of art, and at the age of 76, is a busy entrepreneur who continues to challenge and stretch herself.

Tasha is on a life-long journey of learning, and that includes from the 3 amazing boys in her life. Her two stepsons, Connor Hughes, and Aidan Hughes, continue to demonstrate fortitude, determination, and grace under pressure as they passionately pursue their careers in hockey. They are all-around great people who positively impact those around them. Their youngest brother keeps all of them on their toes with his zany sense of humour, and is Tasha's driving force to living a life of service, passion and purpose.

NATHALIE PLAMONDON-THOMAS

I dream of a world where everybody discovers their full potential @ dnalifecoaching, www.dnalifecoaching.com

"You are more powerful than you know; you are beautiful just as you are." ~ Melissa Etheridge

Nathalie has been a Speaker, Life Coach & Executive Coach for over 10 years and is a No.1 Best Selling Author of several books on wellness and empowerment. She owned and operated a successful printing business for over 10 years with over 50 employees and has over 15 years of experience in sales in the natural food industry. Nathalie combines her sales strengths with the concepts of motivation and the brain programming processes she practices as a Master Practitioner in Neuro Linguistic Programming.

Nathalie was born in a very positive environment. She tells the story about her childhood: "I was born in a small town in Quebec, Canada. You know how a lot of people have [a] story that they suffered in their childhood or had a rough go at something in their life and then they turned their life around, learned from the events and then became stronger? Well, that could not be further away from the truth for me.

"I was raised in a positive and loving environment by highly intelligent and spiritually advanced parents. My parents were really into motivation and positive thinking. And to this day, they are still the most supportive and caring people on the planet. They are my coaches, my friends, my counselors, my fan club and I really look up to them. They wired me to be the person that I am today at a very young age.

In my childhood, they didn't put a gate by the stairs when my brother and I were babies because they never wanted to imply that we could fall. They would instead say: "Be careful around there." They didn't say: "Don't fall" or "Get out of there or you will fall." If they needed me to bring a full glass of water to the table they would just say: "Use a strong steady hand and bring this glass successfully to the table" instead of saying: "Don't spill it!", creating anxiety around the action of carrying the water. Can you see the nuance?

There were signs everywhere in the house with motivational phrases like: "You can be everything you want"; "Yes you can"; "You will miss 100% of the shots you won't take"; "If you're going to do it, do it right"; "There is no luck, you deserve everything you get"; and "Luck is a word that was created by people who are too lazy to do what they have to do". My father's favourite saying was: "NOT ABLE TO is dead, his little sister's name is: TRY."

On Sundays, we were not going to church (although we are Christian Catholics), but instead, my parents would make us sit in the living room to listen to some motivational tape cassettes from Jean-Marc Chaput, Zig Ziglar, Og Mandino, etc. So, needless to say, I was introduced to positive thinking at a very young age."

Nathalie lived in Quebec for a large part of her life. She then moved to Toronto, Ontario in her twenties, where she studied Neuro-Linguistic Programming (NLP) and Life Coaching. She now lives in White Rock, British Columbia where she completed an NLP Master Practitioner Certification with the Robinson Group.

The name of her company is DNA Life Coaching. She believes that everybody has whatever they need inside their DNA in order to obtain, achieve and be whatever they put their mind to. More than a company mission statement, she believes that her life purpose is to motivate and inspire others to be their best.

> *"There are two kinds of people, those who do the work and those who take the credit. Try to be in the first group; there is less competition there."* — *Indira Gandhi*

Nathalie now works with clients one-on-one and helps people become what they want to be. The day she switched her focus from constantly trying to improve her self to helping others discover their full potential, is when she really found her life purpose. To sit in someone's shadow and to watch them shine is so much more rewarding than to shine yourself.

She has also been teaching fitness classes for over 30 years, and is a Nutrition and Wellness Specialist. Fitness and Nutrition have always been her favourite platform in order to help people be their best. She also works with kids in schools, which gives her even wider audience to impact and improve people's lives because she believes if certain values are planted at a young age, they have a better chance to find their roots and flourish.

Nathalie created the THINK Yourself ™ Movement in 2008 with her seminar: THINK Yourself THIN. She realized that it did not matter what area of our life we wanted to improve or wanted to work on. The first step is always between our ears. The way we think influences everything. She created the DNA System, a step-by-step approach to reprogram your brain to be whatever you want to be!

Nathalie's accomplishments include her latest book No.1 Best Seller: *THINK Yourself THIN*, No.1 Best Seller: *Simple Success Strategies*, No.1 Best Seller: *Shine*, her profile featured in the book *Influence*, her many publications in newspapers in Canadian and American media including:

Fox, NBC, KFVS, Travel Weekly, Daily Times Leader, numerous interviews at Influencers Radio, Fuel Radio, Exploring Mind and Body and her complete 2 page profile in the Defyeneurs Magazine, twice, along with many honors in the Fitness Industry including Fitness Instructor of the year for Canada in 2007.

Her unique processes and her inspiring attitude, combined with her energy and contagious smile will empower you to be your best. She has the specialized knowledge and tools to retrain your brain to allow you to take charge of your own life and get inspired from within. *"You can take a horse to water but you can't make him drink"*. Somehow, Nathalie can.

Nathalie dreams of a world where everybody discovers their full potential. Don't Just Be. Be Your Best!